DEEP FAITH

invitation to a deeply rooted life

Dennis R. Atwood

© 2014

Published in the United States by Nurturing Faith Inc., Macon GA, www.nurturingfaith.net.

Library of Congress Cataloging-in-Publication Data is available.

978-1-938514-56-2

All rights reserved. Printed in the United States of America.

Unless otherwise marked, scripture references and quotations are from the New Revised Standard Version Bible, copyright © 1989 National Council of the Churches of Christ in the United States of America. Used by permission. All rights reserved

Scripture quotations marked (NASB) are taken from the New American Standard Bible®, Copyright © 1960, 1962, 1963, 1968, 1971, 1972, 1973, 1975, 1977, 1995 by The Lockman Foundation Used by permission." (www.Lockman.org)

Scripture quotations marked (KJV) are taken from the Holy Bible, King James Version (Public Domain).

For my sons... Dylan, Cole, and Noah.
May your faith grow deeply rooted.

Contents

INTRODUCTION
Deeply Rooted vii

CHAPTER ONE
Desire for Deep Faith 1

CHAPTER TWO
Cultivating Deep Roots 21

CHAPTER THREE
Deep Faith Model 41

CHAPTER FOUR
Formed by Prayer 63

CHAPTER FIVE
Formed by Scripture 85

CHAPTER SIX
Formed by Worship & Community 107

CHAPTER SEVEN
Formed by Missional Service 129

POSTSCRIPT
Sustained by Joy and Grace... 149

LEADER'S GUIDE 153

APPENDIX A
"The Next Seven Days" Journal Guides 185

APPENDIX B
"Order of Meeting" for a Small Group Experience.............. 193

APPENDIX C
Suggestions for Further Reading and Study 195

INTRODUCTION

Deeply Rooted

While most followers of Jesus know that we should be engaged in daily prayer, Scripture reading, worship, fellowship, and ministry, the reality is we often aren't. Life gets in the way. Perhaps we get overwhelmed by the process, or we simply don't see the value in spiritual growth. As a result, church seems shallow and our faith is weak and unattractive to the world.

This book is an attempt to introduce — or reintroduce — ordinary Christians to the core issues vital to personal and corporate spiritual formation. It is for those of us who need a framework, a starting point, or a refresher for engaging in a more intentional and deeper faith. We've all been through times of spiritual drought, doubt, busyness, and crisis. The root issue for folks like us is: *Do I really want to go deeper in my faith — or not?*

Faith in Jesus should be transformative. Faith in Jesus should be vibrant and adventurous! Faith in Jesus should involve the whole person — heart, soul, mind, and strength.

Church *should* be the community where this kind of deep faith is encouraged, nurtured, and modeled in the context of other honest Christ-followers. Church *should* be a safe place where one can be curious, ask questions, share doubts and struggles, and learn to breathe spiritually once again. But all too often it is not.

As a pastor, I have often been guilty of investing too much time in the institutional machinery of church, e.g., attending committees meetings, maintaining church facilities, and putting out fires. At the same time my assumed task is to ensure that every generational group of the church is relatively happy. What is often missing in our (my) frantic attempts to hold the church together in these challenging times is the transformation of individuals (myself) and the larger Christian community itself!

Intuitively, many of us know that we need a deeper, more relevant faith. We need a faith that plunges well beneath the surface of life. We need to allow strong, deep spiritual roots to grow each day that will sustain our life on this earth and bear fruit that lasts into eternity.

A new car, the latest smart phone, a different job, a new relationship, or a trip to the mall won't make us fulfilled and complete. Poking around on the surface of life won't provide meaning. We need to discover — or rediscover — the sacred spiritual practices that cultivate a deep root system of faith for a joyful life.

As deep roots of faith grow, we become transformed into the image of Jesus. Nothing else will ultimately satisfy our souls. In Matthew 11:28-30, Jesus offers an invitation:

> "Come to me, all you that are weary and are carrying heavy burdens, and I will give you rest. Take my yoke upon you, and learn from me; for I am gentle and humble in heart, and you will find rest for your souls. For my yoke is easy, and my burden is light."

Rather than the kind of freedom that avoids ALL yokes and burdens so that we can be free to do whatever we want whenever we want, Jesus tells us the great paradox about freedom is found in submitting our lives under God's reign — *to let our lives become bent toward God's will.*

If you have a gnawing sense that you've been scratching the surface of faith for too long — that something more is needed in your life — then I invite you commit yourself to a deeper faith. These seven chapters are best experienced in the context of community. I encourage you to ask a few friends to join you in this journey. Meet in a coffee shop or start a small group study in your home. We all need others along the pilgrimage toward a deeply rooted life. Deep faith is intensely personal, but it is necessarily communal!

As you begin — or reignite — your spiritual journey, it is important to understand that the ebb and flow of life also applies to faith. A deep faith in Jesus Christ will look a bit different for each one of us as we make our way through the seasons and stages of life. God has created each one of us uniquely.

Teenagers, young adults, parents, and retirees all have different needs and availability of time. Some of us are more contemplative by nature while others are more activity-centered. We have different personality types and learning styles.

Yet even in these complex modern times we can learn from those who have gone before us. Deep faith does not come from a seminar, webcast, or new phone app. Throughout the centuries a "rule of life" (an orderly way of daily experiencing God) has been one proven model for cultivating a deeply rooted life of faith.

The early church also provides another model for deep faith that we will explore later in the book. The way of *grace* assures us that God will meet us wherever we are and take us on an unmatched journey of faith that yields a life deeply rooted in joy and meaning.

In the first two chapters, we will become familiar with what it means to cultivate a deep desire for God and the necessity of building deep spiritual roots.

In the remaining chapters we will examine the early church model of cultivating deep faith that is formed by the sacred spiritual practices of prayer, Scripture, worship, community, and missional service. Ultimately, we will see that the way of deep faith is sustained by a spirit of joy and grace.

At the end of each chapter you will find a section titled "The Next Seven Days." This is crucial! Please don't skip over these pages! Take each daily journal and allow God to cultivate a new rhythm into your life. Seven days for seven weeks — that's the invitation.

Finally, as you work your way through this book, I urge you to be open, honest, and prayerful. Growth that is deep takes time. So, why not pause now and ask God to create in you a clean heart?

Invite God to grant you a hunger and desire for an authentically-deep faith that is rooted in the fullness of God the Trinity. *May you come to know the breadth and depth of God the Father through Jesus Christ in the power of the Holy Spirit who live and reigns, One God, now and forever. AMEN.*

CHAPTER ONE

Desire for a Deep Faith

"Delight yourself in the Lord, and he will give you the desires of your heart." — Psalm 37:4

I.

One hot summer afternoon several years ago, a typical late afternoon thunderstorm rolled into the area of eastern North Carolina where I live. The rain fell with a torrential force, and the winds howled. It was very intense. Then after about 15 minutes, it was all over. When I walked outside I noticed a tree had blown over in my neighbor's front yard across the street. It wasn't a huge tree — maybe 20 feet tall — but it wasn't newly planted either.

It was a Bradford pear tree. Many people fall in love with the rich autumn color and beautiful spring blossoms of the ubiquitous Bradford pear. Bradfords grow fast, and they seem to be planted in just about every new suburban neighborhood. However, Bradford pears are also notorious for having weak wood and shallow root systems. If you're lucky, you might get 25 years out of one these Bradfords.

I walked closer to the fallen tree and was amazed at the lack of roots attached to its base. It was just a clump of dirt with skinny roots sticking out! It reminded me how nature teaches us the important lesson that superficial beauty combined with shallow roots simply will not stand the test of time — or the storms of life.

In contrast to the typical Bradford pear, oak trees tend to live very long lives. One such tree, located on St. John's Island, South Carolina, is known as the Angel Oak tree. It is said to be 1,400 years old!

This tree has massive branches that literally fall to the ground because they are so heavy. Manmade supports have been placed underneath some of these branches to keep them off the ground.

II.

I have a great suspicion that many ordinary folks today have a gnawing in their gut that life could be more. If we are honest, even among many faithful Christians there is often a nagging sense of emptiness. For some of us, the rich spirituality of a living faith in Jesus Christ never developed a deep root system in our lives. As a result, tender shoots of faith have been "rooted out" by something else or blown over in stormy situations.

Such people are living life on the surface — like seeds being blown about by the winds of busyness, ambition, or popular culture. There are simply no roots deep or wide enough in place that can keep surface people connected to the true source of a thriving, fruitful life. Such people may be completely unaware that there is even a root problem — at least, until the storms of life come.

This spiritual sense of *rootlessness* begins to reveal itself with a lack of passion or interest in God and no meaningful connection with a community of faith. People become consumed with making a living, getting through school, or raising a family. Accomplishing goals and moving through the stages of life begin to fly by like mile markers along an Interstate. *And it just happens.*

Whether you call it an unintentional life or a life without proper cultivation, the result is the same: a life lived on the surface desperately in need of a spiritually-deep root system. *So how does one start over? Is there still time for deep roots to be cultivated?*

III.

Kendra Creasy Dean wrote an insightful book based on the findings of the National Study of Youth and Religion (*Almost Christian: What the Faith of Our Teenagers Is Telling the American Church*, Oxford University Press, 2010). In this study, we see:

> . . . a window on how American teenagers have learned a well-intentioned but ultimately banal version of Christianity that's been offered to them in American churches. Most youth seem to accept this bland view of faith as all there is — as something

nice to have, like a bank account, something you have in case you need to draw from it in the future. What Christian adults have not told them is that this account of Christianity is bankrupt. We have not invested in their accounts: we 'teach' young people baseball but we 'expose' them to faith. We provide coaching and opportunities for youth to develop and improve their pitches and SAT scores, but we blithely assume that their religious identity will happen by osmosis and will emerge when 'youth are ready.'[1]

The resulting impact of such a view of faith is either *no faith* or a very shallow faith that rarely sustains or excites. Simply put, the faith of many modern "Christians" is little more than wallpaper on the backdrop of their lives. It's just there. You don't even remember what design or color was on the wall after leaving the room. It's just that underwhelming.

When individual Christians are not deeply rooted in authentic Christian faith, the community called the church becomes limp and shallow. Consequentially, the world is not impacted by the transformational power of Almighty God, because God's power has not transformed our own lives.

The uncomfortable truth is that the lives of today's youth are largely a reflection of — or a reaction against — their parents and other adults around them. Granted, all of us are shaped to a large degree by the families from which we come and the culture in which we live. The good news is that each one of us also possesses the power to open up our lives to a deep faith in God that is real, relevant and robust!

I believe that a great number of Christians today — and those who dabble with church — have a growing sense that there's got to be more to Christian faith than what they have experienced. So, this much we know:

- Deep faith in Christ does not just happen.
- Deep faith is more than church attendance.
- Deep faith is more than simply agreeing that Jesus died to save you from your sins.
- Deep faith must be cultivated.
- Deep faith yields faithful individuals and faithful churches that live out the ways of Christ.

Genuine transformation is desperately needed today! It's so much more than just signing up for a study or discipleship program, getting through it, receiving a certificate, and then saying, "Now I've done that." *Deep faith involves committing your daily life toward cultivating an intentional faith — a lifelong process of being formed into the image of Christ.*

Today's churches desperately need to facilitate the kind of environment that fosters the transformational Gospel of Jesus Christ being set loose in the lives of her members! Churches need to cultivate soil that grows deep healthy roots into Christ who is the head of the church.

I believe that parents, pastors, and other adults who are cultivating a life of deep faith in God *can* impact and nurture a deep faith in the emerging generations. *And in turn, there is much the emerging generations can teach the rest of us about what it means to be people of deep faith in today's world!* ALL people of Christian faith ought to be open and willing to learn from each other and the God who is speaking.

God is at work all around us all the time. We can discover a deep faith in God through intentional and random encounters of grace through the life situations that come our way. The Bible offers us "food that lasts." The church offers us the context of a loving, caring community. The world offers us encounters with the people God created and still passionately loves. When mixed together, the environment right in front of us can become fertile soil for deep roots of faith to grow!

IV.

It all starts with a *desire* to know the God who created you. It grows deeper with a faithful commitment toward the sacred spiritual practices that cultivate roots deep into the soul. And fortunately, it's not all up to us and our achievements. God is the one who brings transformation as we commit to a life dependent upon God's grace. That's it. We don't have to be perfect or just try harder. It all starts with *desire*.

The beginning point is asking God to create in you a sincere deep desire for him. As the Psalmist put it: "Delight yourself in the Lord, and he will give you the desires of your heart" (37:4).

In the Bible the Hebrew words for "desire" (*awah* and *khamadh*) are synonyms "for something understood to be fundamental to human existence." Things like food and water, knowledge, relationships, peace, and a good life.[2] I believe the writers of the Psalms were interested in showing us that basic to our existence and survival is *a delight and desire to know the God who created us.*

There's an old legend about a proud young man who came to Socrates asking for knowledge. He walked up to the muscular philosopher and said, "O great Socrates, I come to you for knowledge." Socrates recognized the young man's selfish motives at once. He led the young man through the streets, to the sea, and chest deep into the water. Then he asked, *"What do you want?"* "Knowledge, O wise Socrates," said the young man with a smile. Socrates put his strong hands on the man's shoulders and pushed him under. Thirty seconds later Socrates let him up. *"What do you want?"* he asked again. "Wisdom," the young man sputtered, "O great and wise Socrates." Socrates plunged him under again. Thirty seconds passed, thirty-five. Forty. Socrates let him up. The man was gasping. *"What do you want, young man?"* Between heavy, heaving breaths the young man wheezed, "Knowledge, O wise and wonderful . . . " Socrates jammed him under again. Forty seconds passed. Fifty. *"What do you want?"* "Air!" he screeched. "I need air!" Socrates replied: *"When you want knowledge as you have just wanted air, then you will have knowledge."*[3]

The Psalmist was declaring that when we come to depend upon God for every breath every moment of every day and delight in God as the Source of our lives, then God will provide what we need when we need it. This is an invitation to a deep, intimate relationship with the God of the Universe. Think about the magnitude and awesome privilege of that invitation!

Now, think about some of the flimsy and familiar reasons why we seem to lack a delight in God and desire for God:

- I'm too busy.
- I'm stressed out.
- I'm overworked.
- I've got financial struggles.
- I honestly don't think about God.
- My life revolves around my family and their expectations.
- My hobbies and recreation are too important to me.
- I'm afraid of going deeper with the call of God.
- I'm afraid of what I may have to give up.

How is it that we make time for personal fitness programs, civic and community organizations, weekly social activities, children's sports activities of every kind such as dance, scouts, etc., and vacations at the beach — just to name a few — but we only give a passing glance to the matter of our relationship with the God who created us, died for us, assures us of resurrection, and daily sustains us?

Think about your life at this present moment. *Do you really desire to have a life with more depth and meaning? Are you honestly growing spiritually? Do you even want to know God and what God desires for your life?*

In Psalm 42:7 we read an interesting and mysterious verse: "Deep calls to deep at the thunder of your cataracts; all your waves and your billows have gone over me."

Could this be a description of the true longing that is within our souls? It may feel like a rock in your shoe that you just can't get rid of — or a gnawing sense of emptiness in your gut. But what if it's actually "deep calling to deep" — the very depth of who God is calling out to meet the very depth of who you are?

The psalmist had a deep passionate desire to know this God who creates and gives life. If you want to connect with that power then you must open up the depths of who you are in order to experience the deep waves of God's love and grace rolling over you. Maybe our greatest problem is that we are so distracted and busy that we just don't understand where to go for life-giving water?

I recently read about an interesting pattern that takes place for animals living in places where water runs in precious short supply. Listen to what farming is like in places that lack an abundant supply of precious water:

> In some farming communities, the farmers might build fences around their properties to keep livestock in and the livestock of neighboring farms out. *This is a bounded set.* But in rural communities where farms or ranches cover an enormous geographic area, fencing the property is out of the question. In (Australia) ranches are so vast that fences are superfluous. Under these conditions a farmer has to sink a bore and create a well, a precious water supply in the Outback. It is assumed that livestock, though they will stray, will never roam too far from the well, lest they die. *This is a centered set.* As long as there is a supply of clean water, the livestock will remain close by.[4]

The question is: *To what, or whom, do you go for your supply of precious life-giving water?* What keeps us coming back to the true Source of life is not a list of rules, coercion or guilt, but rather simple love and trust. There are no rigid boundaries or fences drawn for sheep. There is only the love and trust in the Good Shepherd who will supply all our needs. This a life "centered" on God.

V.

There are many people who consider themselves Christian yet have wandered away from the fold of God's grace. Researchers have termed these people the "de-churched." For a variety of reasons they have become disengaged from a close relationship with God and dropped out of meaningful participation in a faith community. Over time, an increasing number of people have developed a routine of not turning to the true Source of life for nourishment and guidance.

If we are finding refreshment in Christ — which is our deep well — then we will not stray far from him. On the other hand, if we discover that we have strayed away from the well then perhaps we have lost our connection with the Source of our life and we are actually searching for nourishment and fulfillment in other places. Again, Psalm 37:3-5 tells us:

> Trust in the LORD and do good; Dwell in the land and cultivate faithfulness. Delight yourself in the LORD; And He will give you the desires of your heart. Commit your way to the LORD, Trust also in Him, and He will do it. (NASB)

The core issue is one of trust. We either trust in ourselves and the things we can manufacture on our own, or we trust in the Lord of Creation for all our daily life. The avenue for experiencing the reality of God's deep presence is located in "the desires of your heart."

This mechanism for experiencing God's deep presence is activated as we "take delight in the Lord" as a regular pattern for living. This posture represents a relationship flowing with freedom and trust rather than a relationship that is defined by coercion, guilt, and rules.

In order to get the most out of *Deep Faith*, you will need to honestly commit yourself to the daily Scripture readings found in "The Next Seven Days" at the end of each chapter. This is the individual experience that can begin to lead you into the depths of knowing God. *Just try seven minutes, seven days, for seven weeks — not motivated by guilt, but by grace!*

It would be great if you gathered a few friends together and to meet once a week for seven weeks in order to share your insights and honest struggles as you make you're your way through the book. Nevertheless, I urge you to commit yourself to these daily exercises in spiritual formation. *You will be surprised at what God can do with seven good minutes!*

At the heart of *Deep Faith* is a sincere desire and commitment of your individual will to cultivate a life of faithfulness by taking your delight in the Lord. Cultivating faithfulness involves building into the rhythm of your life the sacred spiritual practices of prayer and Scripture, worship and community, and missional service.

When we delight ourselves in God, then God is pleased to grant us the deepest desires of our hearts. Why? Because it is God who molds and shapes our desires. Honestly confronting our true desires is how we begin scratching beneath the surface of life and cultivating the strong roots of a deep faith. There's no point in playing games with God. It won't work.

So how do we begin this quest? For most of us, a "rite of confession" is needed at this point. We must begin by being honest about those things that have dominated our minds, our time, and our energy and return to the deep well — which is Christ Jesus. If that statement applies to your life, then take a moment and read very slowly, honestly, and deliberately the following prayer of confession:

> **Heavenly Father,**
> **forgive me for living my life in such a way that distracts me from knowing you.**
> **I confess that I have become consumed by the cares of this life rather than a desire for the things of your kingdom.**
> **I confess that I have lost a deep desire to know the depths of God my creator and sustainer.**
> **I confess that I have lost my way and need to return to the Source of my life for daily grace and sustenance.**
> **I confess that I need to return to you, O God, and the caring community of your people.**
> **Please guide my steps and enable me to build into the rhythm of my life the sacred practices of prayer and Scripture, worship and community, and missional service with a joyful heart.**
> **Grant me, O God, the desire to know you better, to grow deeper roots of faith, and to participate in the coming of your kingdom on earth as it is in heaven . . .**
> **Through Jesus Christ the Lord, in the power of the Holy Spirit. AMEN.**

THE NEXT SEVEN DAYS

WEEK 1: Desire for a Deep Faith

Over the next seven days, commit yourself toward creating a sacred space in your daily routine in order to read the assigned Scripture, honestly reflect on your life, and pray. This is only the beginning of the journey! Read and pray over the assigned Scripture and begin listening for God. Try seven minutes!

DAY ONE

Read Psalm 37:3-5 slowly two or three times. Don't try to do any more than this during the first week. Write down thoughts or notes as God speaks.

_____
_____
_____
_____
_____
_____
_____
_____
_____

Reflect on the ways that God has been with you recently and in your past, and give thanks to God. Rest in this daily practice — whether it lasts two minutes or ten minutes. This is the beginning of cultivating a new sacred rhythm into your daily life.

_____
_____
_____
_____
_____
_____
_____
_____

Rest. Ask God to create in you a deeper desire to know God — as Father, Son, and Holy Spirit — thereby cultivating a life of deeper faith.

Respond. Write out a prayer of thanksgiving and make a concrete commitment to God for these seven weeks of *Deep Faith* study and spiritual formation.

_____
_____
_____
_____
_____
_____
_____
_____
_____
_____

DAY TWO

Read Psalm 10:17-18 slowly two or three times. Don't try to do any more than this during the first week. Write down thoughts or notes as God speaks.

_____
_____
_____
_____
_____
_____
_____
_____
_____
_____

Reflect on the ways that God has been with you recently and in your past, and give thanks to God. Rest in this daily practice — whether it lasts two minutes or ten minutes. This is the beginning of cultivating a new sacred rhythm into your daily life.

_____
_____
_____
_____
_____
_____
_____
_____
_____

Rest. Ask God to create in you a deeper desire to know God — as Father, Son, and Holy Spirit — thereby cultivating a life of deeper faith.

Respond. Write out a prayer of thanksgiving and make a concrete commitment to God for these seven weeks of *Deep Faith* study and spiritual formation.

_____
_____
_____
_____
_____
_____
_____
_____
_____
_____

DAY THREE

Read Psalm 73:24-26 slowly two or three times. Don't try to do any more than this during the first week. Write down thoughts or notes as God speaks.

_____
_____
_____
_____
_____
_____
_____
_____
_____

Reflect on the ways that God has been with you recently and in your past, and give thanks to God. Rest in this daily practice — whether it lasts two minutes or ten minutes. This is the beginning of cultivating a new sacred rhythm into your daily life.

_____
_____
_____
_____
_____
_____
_____
_____
_____
_____

Rest. Ask God to create in you a deeper desire to know God — as Father, Son, and Holy Spirit — thereby cultivating a life of deeper faith.

Respond. Write out a prayer of thanksgiving and make a concrete commitment to God for these seven weeks of DEEP FAITH study and spiritual formation.

_____
_____
_____
_____
_____
_____
_____
_____
_____
_____
_____
_____

DAY FOUR

Read Psalm 42:1-2 slowly two or three times. Don't try to do any more than this during the first week. Write down thoughts or notes as God speaks.

_____
_____
_____
_____
_____
_____
_____
_____
_____
_____
_____

Reflect on the ways that God has been with you recently and in your past, and give thanks to God. Rest in this daily practice — whether it lasts two minutes or ten minutes. This is the beginning of cultivating a new sacred rhythm into your daily life.

_____
_____
_____
_____
_____
_____
_____
_____
_____

Rest. Close your time by asking God to create in you a deeper desire to know God — as Father, Son, and Holy Spirit — thereby cultivating a life of deeper faith.

Respond. Write out a prayer of thanksgiving and make a concrete commitment to God for these seven weeks of DEEP FAITH study and spiritual formation.

_____
_____
_____
_____
_____
_____
_____
_____
_____

DAY FIVE

Read Psalm 143:6-8 slowly two or three times. Don't try to do any more than this during the first week. Write down thoughts or notes as God speaks.

_____
_____
_____
_____
_____
_____
_____
_____
_____

Reflect on the ways that God has been with you recently and in your past, and give thanks to God. Rest in this daily practice — whether it lasts two minutes or ten minutes. This is the beginning of cultivating a new sacred rhythm into your daily life.

_____
_____
_____
_____
_____
_____
_____
_____
_____

Rest. Close your time by asking God to create in you a deeper desire to know God — as Father, Son, and Holy Spirit — thereby cultivating a life of deeper faith.

Respond. Write out a prayer of thanksgiving and make a concrete commitment to God for these seven weeks of DEEP FAITH study and spiritual formation.

_____
_____
_____
_____
_____
_____
_____
_____
_____
_____

DAY SIX

Read Psalm 63:1 slowly two or three times. Don't try to do any more than this during the first week. Write down thoughts or notes as God speaks.

_____
_____
_____
_____
_____
_____
_____
_____
_____

Reflect on the ways that God has been with you recently and in your past, and give thanks to God. Rest in this daily practice — whether it lasts two minutes or ten minutes. This is the beginning of cultivating a new sacred rhythm into your daily life.

_____
_____
_____
_____
_____
_____
_____
_____
_____
_____

Rest. Close your time by asking God to create in you a deeper desire to know God — as Father, Son, and Holy Spirit — thereby cultivating a life of deeper faith.

Respond. Write out a prayer of thanksgiving and make a concrete commitment to God for these seven weeks of DEEP FAITH study and spiritual formation.

_____
_____
_____
_____
_____
_____
_____
_____
_____

DAY SEVEN

Read Psalm 62:5-6 slowly two or three times. Don't try to do any more than this during the first week. Write down thoughts or notes as God speaks.

_____
_____
_____
_____
_____
_____
_____
_____
_____
_____

Reflect on the ways that God has been with you recently and in your past, and give thanks to God. Rest in this daily practice — whether it lasts two minutes or ten minutes. This is the beginning of cultivating a new sacred rhythm into your daily life.

_____
_____
_____
_____
_____
_____
_____
_____
_____
_____

Rest. Close your time by asking God to create in you a deeper desire to know God — as Father, Son, and Holy Spirit — thereby cultivating a life of deeper faith.

Respond. Write out a prayer of thanksgiving and make a concrete commitment to God for these seven weeks of DEEP FAITH study and spiritual formation.

_____
_____
_____
_____
_____
_____
_____
_____
_____
_____

Notes

[1] Kendra Creasy Dean, *Christian Century*, August 10, 2010:22.

[2] *The New Interpreter's Dictionary of the Bible*, Volume 2. Abingdon Press, Nashville, 2007: 103.

[3] M. Littleton in *Moody Monthly*, June, 1989:29.

[4] Michael Frost and Alan Hirsch, *The Shaping of Things to Come: Innovation and Mission for the 21st Century Church*. Peabody, Mass.: Hendrickson, 2003: 47.

CHAPTER TWO

Cultivating Deep Roots

"As you therefore have received Christ Jesus the Lord, continue to live your lives in him, rooted and built up in him and established in the faith, just as you were taught, abounding with thanksgiving."
— Colossians 2:6-7

I.

When I was a kid growing up in Mississippi, we moved five times when I was between the ages of 5 and 13. That's five different houses in four different towns. Since I married more than twenty-two years ago and began my own family, we have moved six times — six different houses in four different towns in four different states. That's eleven moves — not counting several more I made during my college and graduate school years.

We often refer to moving from one location to another as "uprooting." When we move we pull away from the roots of family, friends, schools, church, athletic teams, and many other familiar places. Of course, the longer we stay in one location, the deeper our roots grow — and the more stuff we accumulate that has to be tossed out or moved once again!

Moving, or *uprooting*, can be quite stressful and traumatic. There are many different reasons for moving, but the hardest part is leaving behind the relationships we have cultivated. The deepest roots in our lives are relational. Leaving behind family and friends is much harder than simply moving your furniture and personal belongings to a different house.

Again, what matters most in our lives are the relationships we have cultivated along the way. And the most important relationship one can ever cultivate is one's relationship to God. Fortunately, when we move from one place to another, we do take our relationship with God with us. In fact it is during those times of being *uprooted* — like a move from one town to another — that we discover just how deeply rooted we are in our relationship with God.

After six experiences in adulthood of being uprooted — so far — I can easily say that my relationship with my wife and three sons has grown stronger and deeper as we have moved and been forced to depend upon God and one another without the comforts of extended family and familiar friends. My relationship with God has also deepened as I have moved out of old comfort zones and routines into relying on God in the new and unfamiliar.

Think about the roots in your own life for a moment. How deep are those roots and where do they run? How would it feel to suddenly be uprooted from all your extended relationships and forced to rely only on the ones that matter most?

In Psalm 1:1-3 we see a picture of the contrast between a life that is deeply rooted and thriving, and a life that is blown about by the influences of the wicked. The differences are quite dramatic.

> Happy are those who do not follow the advice of the wicked, or take the path that sinners tread, or sit in the seat of scoffers; but their delight is in the law of the Lord, and on his law they meditate day and night. They are like trees planted by streams of water, which yield their fruit in its season, and their leaves do not wither. In all they do, they prosper.

Psalm 1 is a wonderful example of the wisdom literature tradition of Israel. The psalmist paints the beautiful word picture of a well-watered tree that is healthy, fruitful, and thriving. In the dry arid regions of Palestine there is very little that grows. But clustered around the sporadic streams that do flow, there is lush green vegetation. This colorful fruitfulness stands out dramatically in such a dry wasteland. This is how the psalmist compares the righteous living in the midst of the wicked.

The lives of the righteous people bear fruit. In fact, their fruit does not wither away. In all they do, their lives *thrive* — which is probably a better translation than "prosper." Unfortunately, when we associate the word "prosper" with God, we may be tempted to think about negative examples of those who preach a "prosperity theology." This misguided "prosperity theology" espouses that God is bound by God's promises to bless us financially and materially if we follow biblical rules or principles — beginning by sending a check to said preacher.

Prospering, or *thriving*, in Psalm 1 is more about the spiritual reality of a person who lives or rests in complete trust and humility before God and neighbor. She is happy and satisfied regardless of the bank account balance, because her delight is in the word and ways of God.

Notice also the contrast between those who are wicked and those who delight in God's law or God's ways. Following the words of the wicked and the pathway of sinners and scoffers leads to a life that has a shallow root system, lacks water, and ultimately withers away. Making poor ethical decisions and chiming in with those who gossip and mock others is a pathway that leads to destruction. When we do these things, over time our lives develop weak and shallow spiritual roots that give way at the slightest drought or wind, crisis or trial.

In ancient farming methods the grain was usually cut and laid on the threshing floor. Next, the grain was thrashed against the floor or beaten with heavy hammers in order to separate the seed heads from the stalks. Finally, a winnowing fork was used to toss the grain into the air where the wind would blow away the outer husks, or chaff, leaving only the grain — which could then be made into bread. The wicked, says the psalmist, are like the chaff that is blown away by the wind.

We all can think of people who have spent the bulk of their lives in pursuit of selfish ambition and instant gratification, unconcerned about anyone else but themselves. We live in a culture that prides itself on personal choice and lifts up the values of autonomy and rugged individualism. To some degree we all have these tendencies within us; however, continually giving in to these desires and allowing them to define our existence ultimately puts us into the classification of "wicked" — according to Psalm 1. This is the essence of living life on the surface.

Like chaff, the wicked will be blown away by the wind. They may have their pleasure, but it is only short-lived and fleeting.

In contrast to the wicked, a person who "delight(s) in the law of the Lord," i.e., God's words and ways, produces a life that is healthy, fruitful, and deeply rooted. The point the psalmist makes is for the necessity of our lives to be intentionally and properly centered in God — our creator and sustainer — rather than toward other "things" which we may be tempted to substitute as the true source of life. Psalm 1 is a wake-up call for God's people to cultivate a deeper life of faith and a more intentional way of living — one that ultimately satisfies and gives meaning — not only to the individual, but also to the world.

II.

In the New Testament, the Apostle Paul says this in his letter to Christians living in Colossae: "As you therefore have received Christ Jesus the Lord, continue to live your lives in him, rooted and built up in him and established in the faith, just as you were taught, abounding with thanksgiving" (Colossians 2:6-7).

If you were fortunate enough to grow up being "rooted and built up" in Christ — with loving Christian parents and a caring church — then you already have in place the deep well of Christ to draw upon. You may or may not be in a regular pattern of intentionally cultivating and strengthening these roots of faith. If you are already in a pattern of cultivating your relationship with God, then perhaps you should examine what that relationship means for you today. If you did not grow up in a setting that encouraged and cultivated your spiritual roots in Christian faith, then how does that affect your life now?

In either case, the relevant question is: *Are you aware of God's active presence in your daily life, or do you simply make it through the day, go to sleep, and get up to do it all over again?*

In other words, is faith for you an active daily part of life or is it something that is passive and deactivated most days? Is your faith a noun or a verb? Notice the verbs mentioned in Colossians 2:6-7 that describe a deeply rooted faith in Christ.

- Received
- Continue
- Rooted
- Built
- Established
- Taught
- Abounding

Many people typically think of faith as a noun rather than a verb. In this sense, faith is something that you "have" or possess as a "thing." When faith is viewed as a noun, it is most often understood as a set of beliefs to which you intellectually ascend or agree; however, the biblical idea of faith paints the picture of a person throwing one's life into something or someone. It is "believing" in the sense of acting upon rather than simply agreeing with.

During his life of earth, Jesus would often say to a person that he had just healed: ". . . your faith has made you well" (Matthew 9:24). As far as I know, Jesus never asked a sick person to fill out a questionnaire or answer three questions correctly about God before he healed them. Jesus looked at the heart of the individual and saw the true desires of the people he encountered. Faith is not something we can fake with God!

Hebrews 11 offers a descriptive litany about faith: "Now faith is the assurance of things hoped for, the conviction of things not seen" (v.1). Then the author goes on to offer real life examples of the actions of Abel, Enoch, Noah, Abraham, Isaac, Jacob, Joseph, Moses, the Israelite people, Rahab, and many others. All of these people acted upon a belief in God to the point that they literally committed their lives toward some kind of concrete action on God's behalf.

So biblical faith involves the whole person — not just the intellect. Thus every aspect of our lives is affected by faith. Christian faith cannot be separated from the other aspects of one's life. Following Jesus is pervasive. He touches everything. Therefore authentic faith in Jesus — following Jesus — means that you must be inextricably connected to him!

The Greek word used in Colossians 2 for *rooted* refers to a tree with roots spreading deep into the soil. So here's the clincher: *the secret to a life that thrives or prospers* (in the words of the Psalmist) *and the person who is established in the faith* (in the words of the Apostle Paul) *is what you cannot see!*

The beautiful leaves are not the most important part of the tree. Rather, it is the root system that is hidden beneath the surface! Even the leaves of a healthy oak tree fall once a year and blow away, but the roots system remains. The most beautiful part of a healthy tree — and every person — is actually what lies beneath the surface!

III.

In the Gospel of John 15:1-8, Jesus gives us an even more vivid perspective of this image of cultivating deep roots of faith. He tells the disciples:

> "I am the true vine, and my Father is the vinegrower. He removes every branch in me that bears no fruit. Every branch that bears fruit he prunes to make it bear more fruit. You have already been cleansed by the word that I have spoken to you.
>
> Abide in me as I abide in you. Just as the branch cannot bear fruit by itself unless it abides in the vine, neither can you unless you abide in me. I am the vine, you are the branches. Those

who abide in me and I in them bear much fruit, because apart from me you can do nothing.

Whoever does not abide in me is thrown away like a branch and withers; such branches are gathered, thrown into the fire, and burned.

If you abide in me, and my words abide in you, ask for whatever you wish, and it will be done for you. My Father is glorified by this, that you bear much fruit and become my disciples."

The purpose of Jesus' analogy is to describe the abiding relationship between himself and his follower(s) likened to that earlier relationship between Yahweh and Israel. In Psalm 80:8-11 we hear a familiar metaphor: "You brought a vine out of Egypt; you drove out the nations and planted it. You cleared the ground for it; it took deep root and filled the land. The mountains were covered with its shade, the mighty cedars with its branches; it sent out its branches to the sea, and its shoots to the River."

God was committed to Israel. God preserved the people. God brought them out of captivity and planted them in a fertile land. Then God wanted them to cultivate deep roots of faith in this Promised Land. God wanted God's people to continue to depend on God for everything.

As with Israel, the connection between the true vine and the branch is essential for the life of God's people and intended to bear fruit. "Abide in me," Jesus says, meaning abide in my *love. Become deeply connected with my love in a relationship of close communion.*

But notice the attachment of the two parties — the vine and branch — is not viewed as an end in itself. Rather, the purpose of the attachment is to remain connected to one another and, *as a natural result*, to "bear fruit." How can we do this?

The *bond* with Christ is maintained by abiding in him and his words (historically Scripture and the teachings of Jesus) through the church and through the Holy Spirit in your interior life. Notice how the phrases "I am" and "you are" are reiterated for emphasis to show there is a mutual abiding that results in much fruit. Here fruit may be understood as qualities of a Christ-follower's character as well as the effect of one's life upon others.

Notice also that when the connection between vine and branch is broken the result is NO fruit. Nothing. At the end of the day, the entire relationship stands under both grace (v.3) and judgment (v.6).

Think about it. *What do you do with broken-off branches that become scattered around your yard?* If you're like me, then you gather them up and either burn them or throw them away. So Jesus makes a point to emphasize the necessity and seriousness of remaining in vital connection with him if fruitfulness is to result and continue.

Let's be honest — mustering up the desire to know Christ on a daily basis can be a challenge. Life is busy. Between work, school, raising kids and driving them to dozens of activities every week, caring for aging parents, participating in community activities, keeping up with chores at home, having some kind of a social life, and hopefully going to church, life can a bit overwhelming. But Jesus is trying to tell us we cannot do anything in our own strength — at least nothing that will last.

You see, we can build pretty lives that look attractive and successful on the outside while we are actually wasting away beneath the surface. We can also build shiny, sparkly churches that appear to be "relevant" and growing, or "rich with tradition," but are essentially rootless and spiritually weak beneath the surface.

What is clear is that we cannot neglect to become more deeply rooted in our relationship with God in Christ if our personal lives and the work of our churches is to last. So how do we begin to "abide in Christ" and cultivate deep roots of faith?

It takes intentionality and a willingness to dig deep and get a little dirty. Deep faith does not just happen one day when we are "ready," or when we have more time, or when everything suddenly falls in place. As we will explore in the chapters to come, this intentional process of spiritual formation involves *prayer, Scripture, worship, community*, and *missional service.*

It all starts with a desire to know God and cultivate deep roots of faith which is itself a gift of God's grace. If you will be honest about your desire, then God will honor that. If your desire for other things is stronger than your desire to know God, then you can ask God to change your desire.

Yet a desire must ultimately lead to a faith put into action — a daily and weekly commitment to make your ways God's ways. *Would you expect to have a great crop of fresh vegetables to eat if you simply went outside, dug a few dinky holes, and randomly threw out some seeds?*

Of course not! It takes time and daily commitment. First you would select a piece of land that is fertile and rich; you would come and till or plow up the soil. Then you would carefully plant the seeds and come back every day to make sure those seeds have enough water. You would even come from time to time and pull the weeds that threaten to choke out the good seeds. Finally, after much care and patience, you would experience the joy of seeing the fruits of your labor — and most importantly, you would get to eat those fresh vegetables!

That's why these seven days for seven weeks are so important to your faith. These 49 days can literally cultivate a new pattern or rhythm into your way of life! None of us will ever reach perfection, but we can learn how to be sustained by God's grace and live a life that is thriving and fruitful. God sees your heart. God knows if your honest desire is to love him and follow Christ.

The desire to know God and to grow a deeper faith is itself a gift of God's grace, and God will honor your desire. The words of this liberating prayer of deep faith from Thomas Merton offer us honest hope and encouragement for the way forward . . .

> **My Lord God, I have no idea where I am going. I do not see the road ahead of me. I cannot know for certain where it will end.**
> **Nor do I really know myself, and the fact that I think I am following your will does not mean that I am actually doing so.**
> **But I believe that the desire to know you does in fact please you. And I hope that I have that desire in all that I am doing.**
> **And I know that if I do this you will lead me by the right road; even though, I may know nothing about it.**
> **Therefore, I will trust you always. Though I may seem to be lost and in the shadow of death; I will not fear, for you are with me.**
> **And you will never leave me to face my perils alone. AMEN.** [1]

THE NEXT SEVEN DAYS

WEEK 2: Cultivating Deep Roots

Over the next seven days, commit yourself toward making a sacred spiritual space in your daily routine in order to read the assigned Scripture, honestly reflect over your life, and pray.

DAY ONE

Begin your sacred time with a few minutes of silence. Try to clear your mind and breathe deeply.

Read Psalm 1:1-3 and listen for God. Read the Scripture passage slowly two or three times. Write down thoughts or notes as God speaks to you. What words seem to jump off the page at you?

_____

_____

_____

_____

_____

_____

_____

Reflect on the ways that God has been with you recently and in your past, and give thanks to God. Rest in this daily practice — whether it lasts two minutes or ten minutes. Enjoy these quiet moments. You are cultivating a new sacred rhythm into your daily life.

_____

_____

_____

_____

_____

_____

_____

Rest. Ask God to create in you a deeper desire to know God and cultivate a deeply rooted faith.

Respond. Write out a weekly and daily strategy for creating sacred spiritual space to commune with God. Recommit yourself toward weekly and daily spiritual formation.

_____
_____
_____
_____
_____
_____
_____
_____
_____

DAY TWO

Begin your sacred time with a few minutes of silence. Try to clear your mind and breathe deeply.

Read Jeremiah 17:7-8 and listen for God. Read the Scripture passage slowly two or three times. Write down thoughts or notes as God speaks to you. What words seem to jump off the page at you?

_____
_____
_____
_____
_____
_____
_____
_____

Reflect on the ways that God has been with you recently and in your past, and give thanks to God. Rest in this daily practice — whether it lasts two minutes or ten minutes. Enjoy these quiet moments. You are cultivating a new sacred rhythm into your daily life.

_____
_____
_____
_____
_____
_____
_____
_____
_____

Rest. Ask God to create in you a deeper desire to know God and cultivate a deeply rooted faith.

Respond. Reaffirm your weekly and daily strategy for creating sacred spiritual space in order to commune with God. Be flexible enough to make adjustments as you go along the path of weekly and daily spiritual formation.

_____
_____
_____
_____
_____
_____
_____
_____
_____
_____

DAY THREE

Begin your sacred time with a few minutes of silence. Try to clear your mind and breathe deeply.

Read Isaiah 11:1-10 and listen for God. Read the Scripture passage slowly two or three times. Write down thoughts or notes as God speaks to you. What words seem to jump off the page at you?

_____
_____
_____
_____
_____
_____
_____
_____
_____
_____

Reflect on the ways that God has been with you recently and in your past, and give thanks to God. Rest in this daily practice — whether it lasts two minutes or ten minutes. Enjoy these quiet moments. You are cultivating a new sacred rhythm into your daily life.

_____
_____
_____
_____
_____
_____
_____
_____

Rest. Ask God to create in you a deeper desire to know God and cultivate a deeply rooted faith.

Respond. Reaffirm your weekly and daily strategy for creating sacred spiritual space in order to commune with God. Be flexible enough to make adjustments as you go along the path of weekly and daily spiritual formation.

_____
_____
_____
_____
_____
_____
_____
_____
_____
_____

DAY FOUR

Begin your sacred time with a few minutes of silence. Try to clear your mind and breathe deeply.

Read Colossians 2:6-7 and begin listening for God. Read the Scripture passage slowly two or three times. Write down thoughts or notes as God speaks to you. What words seem to jump off the page at you?

_____
_____
_____
_____
_____
_____
_____
_____

Reflect on the ways that God has been with you recently and in your past, and give thanks to God. Rest in this daily practice — whether it lasts two minutes or ten minutes. Enjoy these quiet moments. You are cultivating a new sacred rhythm into your daily life.

_____
_____
_____
_____
_____
_____
_____
_____
_____
_____

Rest. Ask God to create in you a deeper desire to know God and cultivate a deeply rooted faith.

Respond. Reaffirm your weekly and daily strategy for creating sacred spiritual space in order to commune with God. Be flexible enough to make adjustments as you go along the path of weekly and daily spiritual formation.

_____
_____
_____
_____
_____
_____
_____
_____
_____
_____

DAY FIVE

Begin your sacred time with a few minutes of silence. Try to clear your mind and breathe deeply.

Read Matthew 13:3-9 and listen for God. Read the Scripture passage slowly two or three times. Write down thoughts or notes as God speaks to you. What words seem to jump off the page at you?

_____
_____
_____
_____
_____
_____
_____
_____

Reflect on the ways that God has been with you recently and in your past, and give thanks to God. Rest in this daily practice — whether it lasts two minutes or ten minutes. Enjoy these quiet moments. You are cultivating a new sacred rhythm into your daily life.

_____
_____
_____
_____
_____
_____
_____
_____

Rest. Ask God to create in you a deeper desire to know God and cultivate a deeply rooted faith.

Respond. Reaffirm your weekly and daily strategy for creating sacred spiritual space in order to commune with God. Be flexible enough to make adjustments as you go along the path of weekly and daily spiritual formation.

DAY SIX

Begin your sacred time with a few minutes of silence. Try to clear your mind and breathe deeply.

Read John 15:4-5 and listen for God. Read the Scripture passage slowly two or three times. Write down thoughts or notes as God speaks to you. What words seem to jump off the page at you?

Reflect on the ways that God has been with you recently and in your past, and give thanks to God. Rest in this daily practice — whether it lasts two minutes or ten minutes. Enjoy these quiet moments. You are cultivating a new sacred rhythm into your daily life.

_____
_____
_____
_____
_____
_____
_____
_____
_____
_____

Rest. Close your time by asking God to create in you a deeper desire to know God and cultivate a deeply rooted faith.

Respond. Reaffirm your weekly and daily strategy for creating sacred spiritual space in order to commune with God. Be flexible enough to make adjustments as you go along the path of weekly and daily spiritual formation.

_____
_____
_____
_____
_____
_____
_____
_____
_____
_____

DAY SEVEN

Begin your sacred time with a few minutes of silence. Try to clear your mind and breathe deeply.

Read Ephesians 3:16-17 and listen for God. Read the Scripture passage slowly two or three times. Write down thoughts or notes as God speaks to you. What words seem to jump off the page at you?

_____
_____
_____
_____
_____
_____
_____
_____
_____
_____

Reflect on the ways that God has been with you recently and in your past, and give thanks to God. Rest in this daily practice — whether it lasts two minutes or ten minutes. Enjoy these quiet moments. You are cultivating a new sacred rhythm into your daily life.

_____
_____
_____
_____
_____
_____
_____
_____
_____
_____

Rest. Ask God to create in you a deeper desire to know God and cultivate a deeply rooted faith.

Respond. Reaffirm your weekly and daily strategy for creating sacred spiritual space in order to commune with God. Be flexible enough to make adjustments as you go along the path of weekly and daily spiritual formation.

_____
_____
_____
_____
_____
_____
_____
_____
_____
_____

Notes
[1] *Thoughts in Solitude*, Part Two, Chapter II consists of fifteen lines that have become known as "The Merton Prayer." Farrar, Straus, & Giroux: New York.1956,1958:77.

CHAPTER THREE

The Deep Faith Model

"They devoted themselves to the apostles' teaching and fellowship, to the breaking of bread and the prayers. Awe came upon everyone, because many wonders and signs were being done by the apostles. All who believed were together and had all things in common; they would sell their possessions and goods and distribute the proceeds to all, as any had need. Day by day, as they spent much time together in the temple, they broke bread at home and ate their food with glad and generous hearts, praising God and having the goodwill of all the people. And day by day the Lord added to their number those who were being saved." — Acts 2:42-47

I.

During the first two chapters, we have considered our individual desire for God and the need to personally cultivate deep roots of faith into our lives. But now it's time to admit that we cannot do it alone. Christian faith was meant to be lived out in the context of community — also known as the church.

Someone has said: *Jesus came preaching the kingdom of God, and people created the church!* I'm not willing to presume that God didn't have anything to do with the creation of the church, but I get the point. We are flawed human matter — a mixture of molecules, DNA, and flesh. We who have come to faith in Jesus Christ are still sinners in need of God's grace, and it often shows up in our life together as the church.

It's very unfortunate that there are many people today who have decided they don't want to have anything to do with God because of bad experiences with the church and those who claim the name "Christian."

In a report titled, "American Religion: Contemporary Trends," we find another indicator that America's congregations are shrinking and people are thinking less about faith. The author of the study, Mark Chaves, concludes that over the last generation religious belief in America has experienced a "softening" in which far more people are willing to say they don't belong to any religious tradition than in the past.

Using data from over the past forty years, as many as 20 percent of all Americans today say they don't belong to any religious group compared to just 3 percent in the 1950s. Yet, 92 percent claim a belief in God.

Researcher Bradley Wright says, "Forty or 50 years ago, it was almost a form of deviance not to be religious." Chaves says these trends developed slowly and he doesn't think they can be reversed by ramped up evangelism or other efforts. The study also reported that older people are more likely to be religious than the young, and that immigrants also tend to be active religious believers. Whether you call it a shift or a decline, the religious landscape has changed greatly over the past several decades in North America. People are more willing to leave the faith and traditions in which they were raised and changing demographics have certainly played a major factor in the decline of faith.[1]

This study is just one more signal that we in the church must reach deep into our faith and make it real in our own lives before we can offer a faith with substance to the growing numbers of disinterested and disenfranchised people with whom we live and work each day.

The truth is we seldom hear of good, healthy congregations modeling for us how to be the church today. Times change, structures change, technologies change, and we human beings are inevitably going to fail and fall. But it's by the way we *love one another*, Jesus says, that the world will know we are his disciples (John 13:35).

How we forgive one another and pray, how we dedicate our lives to the worship of God, how we follow the ways of God's Word, how we give of ourselves in service to others — especially to the poor and disenfranchised — all these things matter. *Yet it is how we love that matters most!*

There never has been or never will be a Christian version of Disneyworld where all is right and good, clean and just. We simply don't live in that kind of world — at least not yet. The "good ol' days" that each generation talks about were probably never as good as we remember them.

We live in real time in the real world as it is today. That's all we have to work with. Romanticizing the past or fantasizing about the future won't do one thing to help us today.

Yet there is an ancient real life model we can look to and learn from when it comes to the matter of how to become an authentic community of Christ-followers. Warning: it will do us no good to romanticize the first-century model of church either, but there are some clear-cut principles we can see being enacted in the early stages of the Christian movement.

This ancient model shows us a lively, vibrant community of people practicing deep faith. The model would be tested, splintered, and over time evolve into a variety of forms. But the essence of the faith we see in the ancient church model is still a healthy model of deep faith for us to pattern our lives after today.

II.

It is said that St. Francis of Assisi was out hoeing his garden one day when someone asked what he would do if he were to suddenly learn that he would die before sunset that very day. St. Francis said, "I would finish hoeing my garden." That is the perspective of someone who is very secure in the fact that he is living out God's vision for his life in every moment that God gives him. St. Francis was "fully present" with God!

Contrast this with the less likely story of the woman who came rushing to the preacher saying, "That woman over there says she just saw a vision of Jesus at the altar! What should we do?" The pastor replied, "Look busy!"

When it comes to your experience of church, are you secure in the thought that your church is doing exactly what God wants it to be doing fulfilling God's vision for the church? Or is your experience more like that preacher's pitiful advice that we should try and look busy when we get the feeling that God is really paying attention?

Just what should the church look like? And where is our model for the ideal church? That's a question that has as many answers as there are people in any given congregation. And that's why church life can get a little messy at times.

It reminds me of the welcome sign you see as you drive into the tiny community of Puckett, Mississippi, which says, "Welcome to Puckett, 300 Good, Friendly Folks and a Few Old Soreheads."

That's a welcome sign you don't forget, and it's an honest assessment of a typical community of people! However, it does raise some interesting questions like, "Just who are these soreheads? Did the town take a vote? Do these soreheads go to church? If so, are they Baptist, Methodist, Roman Catholic, or some other fortunate denomination? Are these soreheads primarily men or women, young or old?" *Chances are the answer is . . . all of the above.*

Here's my point. Just as I am asking you to be honest about where you are right now in your personal desires for God versus other things, we must also be honest when it comes to our life together as Christ's church. The truth is congregations are a lot like small communities. For the most part, they're filled with good, loving, friendly Christian folks. But we do live in a society that is filled with soreheads, whiners, and generally unhealthy people. So we should expect to have our fair share in our congregations — maybe even more than our fair share! After all, the church is a place for sinners just as a hospital is a place for sick people. But let's go back to the question: *What is the model of the ideal church?*

The first phase of the "Unbinding the Gospel" series, a study sponsored by the Lilly Foundation, identified characteristics of growing mainline churches. They learned that growing congregations did not fit a political or theological profile; some were unabashedly conservative and others were unabashedly liberal. Surprisingly, they discovered that growing churches were not the congregations that talked the most about evangelism. The study found that growing congregations had three things in common:

1) The members had a vivid, life-giving spiritual life.
2) The members felt comfortable talking about their spiritual life with one another.
3) The congregation was not focused inward, but outward toward their community. [2]

Deep faith works from the inside out. It is a matter of getting healthy and balanced inwardly before lasting outward growth can occur. Yet, many churches today suffer from "spiritual anemia." They have no vision, no sense of direction, and they're often filled with division and conflict. Such churches often live by the "wisdom of this world" rather than the "wisdom of God," as James put it.

It was within a context of unhealthy church life and "spiritual anemia" that James the Apostle addressed a similar question. James wrote to tell early Christians that what they do and how they treat one another does matter! His solution for this unhealthy congregation was for its members to quit relying on wisdom that is earthly, unspiritual, and devilish, and to start relying on the "wisdom from above" which he then describes:

> But the wisdom from above is first pure, then peaceable, gentle, willing to yield, full of mercy and good fruits, without a trace of partiality or hypocrisy. And a harvest of righteousness is sown in peace for those who make peace. (James 3:17-18)

This "wisdom from above" stands in stark contrast from the preceding and following verses that mention such unhealthy characteristics being displayed in that congregation as: bitter envy; selfish ambition; unspiritual, earthly, devilish disorder; wickedness; conflicts; and disputes — not exactly the qualities of a growing church!

So, James supplied "eight characteristics for developing a healthy, vibrant community of faith that are supplied by the wisdom from above." They can be summarized by eight adjectives James uses to describe the kind of people who make up a healthy vibrant community of faith: pure, peaceable, considerate, open-minded, compassionate, helpful, straightforward, and sincere. Sounds great, doesn't it?

Now, it's important to note that James was written late in the first-century, years after the church had been birthed, years removed from the glowing unity and mutual love of the those first Christian communities in the Book of Acts. And herein lies the point.

I believe that in the beginning the earliest Christians were asking the right question: "What is God's vision for the Church or for followers of the Way?" But as time went on, Christians began to ask, "What is our vision for the church?"

Let's take a poll or conduct focus groups and then we'll determine by majority vote the right vision for the church — for our church. This question is, of course, the wrong question. It's not a matter of what I want, what you want, or what a coalition in the church wants. The question is about what God wants. So, in order to find our Deep Faith model, we must go back to the earliest days of the church and seek to discover God's vision for how to be Christ's body on mission in the world today.

III.

But before we look at the *Deep Faith* model, there are at least two things that ought to unite followers of Jesus when we seek God's vision for the Church. First, we should be committed to the Church because God is. But it would naïve to think that we are all committed to the Church. The typical congregation averages only about one-third of its total membership who are active participants. Sometimes Christians who don't get their way drop out of their church. Sometimes Christians get their feelings hurt and drop out of their church. Sometimes Christians get lazy and drop out of their church. Sometimes Christians simply get too busy and they quit being involved in the life of their church. There are many reasons or excuses that Christians give for not being committed to Christ's Church.

However, there is no such thing in the New Testament as an "unchurched" Christian. It may sound nice and spiritual to be interested in Jesus but not the church, but the fact is we can't have one without the other. To be committed to Christ is to be committed to the body of Christ. The Church lies at the very center of God's work in the world today, and the Church is the very body of Christ himself.

God's eternal purpose that is being worked out in history and will be perfected one day in the future is not just to save isolated individuals and keep us in our independent lonely state. The purpose of God has always been to set apart a people. The Church, as a people, did not actually begin on the Day of Pentecost. The concept of the Church as the people of God goes all the way back to Abraham, when God promised to bless all the nations through him. This would become partially realized through the people of Israel, but not fully. At Pentecost, the remnant of God's people became the spirit-filled Body of Christ.

So we should understand that God's vision for the Church is to call out a people for himself who will live the alternative values of God's kingdom and continue the mission of Jesus in the world. The primary reason we should be committed to the Church is because God is committed to the Church as God's own people in the world today.

We also should be committed to the Church because churches today desperately need transformation. In many parts of the third-world, churches are growing and spreading rapidly. In America there are some churches that are growing rapidly — at least on the surface — but there are many more that are declining steadily. Yet in both cases, there is an abundance of superficial spirituality in the North American church.

Where is the passion for going deeper in our faith in Christ and in being his body in the world? Where is the passion for making tangible commitments to justice and peace and equality? The truth is there's more interest in what the church can do for me than in what I can do to help the church fulfill God's vision in the world today — yet another byproduct of living in a consumeristic society.

In another study we see this evidence showing up in our giving and spending habits. According to "The State of Church Giving through 2009," tithing to mainline Protestant churches is at its lowest level in at least 41 years. During 2009, parishioners gave about 2.38 percent of their income to the church, and of that income only 0.34 percent went toward "benevolences" such as charities and ministries beyond the walls of the church. To put it another way, of the lower receipts that American churches are receiving, they are spending more on themselves and less on causes beyond the church's operating expenses.[3] God remains committed to the church, yet the church desperately needs transformation — not a new gimmick or program!

IV.

So where do we find our Deep Faith model? To answer that question we need to go back to the earliest days of the Church in Jerusalem. But we will look at it through rose colored glasses if we don't acknowledge that the Church has always had it faults. There were rivalries, hypocrisies, immoralities, and heresies that plagued the early Church just as they continue to plague the Church of the 21st century.

But there is one thing that is clear — the early Church, despite its problems and failures, had been radically transformed by the Holy Spirit. So we come back to the question: What did the early Church look like and what evidences did it give of the presence and power of the Holy Spirit? If we can find some answers to this question, then we can be well on our way to discovering an authentic model of deep faith for the Church in the 21st century.

I conclude this chapter with an overview of tangible marks of the Deep Faith model, and then I will examine each one of them more carefully throughout the remainder of the book. The story of the early Church, as described in the Book of Acts, is not so much about the stars of the movement like Peter and Paul and Barnabas. Instead, the focal point in the Book of Acts is the community of believers the Holy Spirit was forming and shaping. Their relationships are at the core of the early Church. The ancient Church in the Book of Acts is the model of a missional community engaged in a deep faith in God through Jesus Christ, sustained and guided by the power of the Holy Spirit.

There are five forming principals of that early Christian community of disciples. Their genuinely-deep faith was formed by the Holy Spirit through these five clearly-identifiable actions or experiences in Acts 2. I will refer to them as sacred spiritual practices that form us and provide the crucial nutrients for deep roots of faith.

Prayer. Our faith is formed as individuals and in the context of community through the practice of abiding in Christ, also known as prayer. There are many ways in which we can pray. I will say more later about various forms of prayer, but for now, I invite you to honestly ask yourself: What does prayer mean for me today? And how can I be more intentional in cultivating a deeper life of prayer?

Scripture. Our faith is formed by the words of Holy Scripture. The early Christians were "devoted" to the Apostle's teaching. The Greek word *proskartereo* means "to be devoted to, to continue in, to be strong towards." These ancient Christians were hungry for the word of God; they were strongly committed to continuing in and learning from the Scripture. Having a proper view of Scripture, and being devoted to how it shapes and forms us, is essential for a deep faith. This involves the regular habit of asking questions and honestly seeking to go deeper into the teachings of Scripture and its applications for our lives (Acts 2:42). So ask yourself: What does the Bible mean for me today? And how can I cultivate a desire for a deeper engagement with Scripture?

Worship. Our faith is formed by gathering with fellow disciples for the regular worship of the Triune God. Authentic worship forms deep faith within us when we gather together for the purpose of experiencing God's presence. Ask yourself: What does worship mean to me today? How can I open myself to a deeper experience of God through the rich variety of worship that is available?

Community. Our faith is formed by the Holy Spirit's work of koinonia (Gk.) — or fellowship — community in the life of all believers. This kind of community is different than other groups in society. New Testament community involves the honest acceptance of others, the equal sharing in grace at the table as we break bread together, and working towards the common good of all. Ask yourself: What does being in community with other Christians mean to me today? How might I need to deepen my experience of Christian community?

Missional Service. We are also formed by our missional service to all who have need. God is a "sending" missional God and we are God's "sent" missional people. The outward focus of service to others was a sign of early Christian's unity with one another and a commitment to the common good of all. A deep faith in Christ involves working for justice and equality, caring for the forgotten or neglected, giving sacrificially for those in need, and sharing our spiritual gifts as we live out our lives and careers in the world. Ask yourself: In what ways do I need to bend the focus of my life away from myself and toward others? Who are some people in my community that I need to serve?

Prayer, Scripture, worship, community, and missional service are the forming principles of the ancient church that provide for us a biblical model for deep faith.

V.

John Stott wrote about a group of Christian students to whom he was introduced several years ago in the capital city of a Latin American country. These were students who had dropped out of churches. They called themselves Christianos Descolgados, meaning "unhooked Christians."

They said they had visited every church in their city and had been unable to find what they were looking for. When asked what it was they were looking for, they said they were looking for a church where:

1) The Bible was taught,
2) There was a loving and caring fellowship,
3) There was sincere and humble worship,
4) There was a compassionate outreach to the world outside.[4]

Sounds like those students were looking for a church that resembled the deep faith model of the early Church described in the Book of Acts! We have a biblical model for how Jesus intends us to live as his followers. We know the basic nutrients that are needed for deep roots of faith to grow healthy and strong. This will be our focus in the coming chapters as we seek to cultivate the roots of *Deep Faith*.

Holy God,
You have always had a people, beginning with Israel and now through your church.

Although we are imperfect and weak, help us to bear with one another, forgiving one another and loving one another with Jesus Christ as our model.

Together we are Christ's body, and he is the living head of the Church in the power of the Holy Spirit. AMEN.

THE NEXT SEVEN DAYS

WEEK 3: The Deep Faith Model

Over the next seven days commit yourself toward the practice of making a sacred spiritual space in your daily routine in order to read the assigned Scripture, honestly reflect over your life, and pray.

DAY ONE

Begin your sacred time with a few minutes of silence. Try to clear your mind and breathe deeply.

Read Acts 2:42-47 and listen for God. Read the Scripture passage slowly two or three times. Write down thoughts or notes as God speaks to you. What words seem to jump off the page at you?

_____
_____
_____
_____
_____
_____
_____

Reflect on the ways that God has been with you recently and in your past, and give thanks to God. Rest in this daily practice. Try to build your time up to 15 minutes. Enjoy these quiet moments. You are cultivating deeper roots into the rhythm of your daily life.

_____
_____
_____
_____
_____
_____
_____

Rest. Close your time by asking God to create in you a desire to know God in a deeper relationship.

Respond. Write down how God wants you to respond to today's Scripture reading and incorporate this learning into your life. Also, consider God's vision for the church and how you fit into the Body of Christ.

_____
_____
_____
_____
_____
_____
_____
_____
_____

DAY TWO

Begin your sacred time with a few minutes of silence. Try to clear your mind and breathe deeply.

Read Acts 4:31 and listen for God. Read the Scripture passage slowly two or three times. Write down thoughts or notes as God speaks to you. What words seem to jump off the page at you?

_____
_____
_____
_____
_____
_____
_____
_____
_____

Reflect on the ways that God has been with you recently and in your past, and give thanks to God. Rest in this daily practice. Try to build your time up to 15 minutes. Enjoy these quiet moments. You are cultivating deeper roots into the rhythm of your daily life.

_____
_____
_____
_____
_____
_____
_____
_____
_____
_____

Rest. Ask God to create in you a desire to know God in a deeper relationship.

Respond. Write down how God wants you to respond to today's Scripture reading and incorporate this learning into your life. Also, consider God's vision for the church and how you fit into the Body of Christ.

_____
_____
_____
_____
_____
_____
_____
_____
_____
_____

DAY THREE

Begin your sacred time with a few minutes of silence. Try to clear your mind and breathe deeply.

Read Acts 4:32-35 and listen for God. Read the Scripture passage slowly two or three times. Write down thoughts or notes as God speaks to you. What words seem to jump off the page at you?

_____
_____
_____
_____
_____
_____
_____
_____

Reflect on the ways that God has been with you recently and in your past, and give thanks to God. Rest in this daily practice. Try to build your time up to 15 minutes. Enjoy these quiet moments. You are cultivating deeper roots into the rhythm of your daily life.

_____
_____
_____
_____
_____
_____
_____
_____

Rest. Ask God to create in you a desire to know God in a deeper relationship.

Respond. Write down how God wants you to respond to today's Scripture reading and incorporate this learning into your life. Also, consider God's vision for the church and how you fit into the Body of Christ.

_____
_____
_____
_____
_____
_____
_____
_____
_____
_____

DAY FOUR

Begin your sacred time with a few minutes of silence. Try to clear your mind and breathe deeply.

Read Acts 8:35-38 and listen for God. Read the Scripture passage slowly two or three times. Write down thoughts or notes as God speaks to you. What words seem to jump off the page at you?

_____
_____
_____
_____
_____
_____
_____
_____

Reflect on the ways that God has been with you recently and in your past, and give thanks to God. Rest in this daily practice. Try to build your time up to 15 minutes. Enjoy these quiet moments. You are cultivating deeper roots into the rhythm of your daily life.

_____
_____
_____
_____
_____
_____
_____
_____
_____
_____

Rest. Ask God to create in you a desire to know God in a deeper relationship.

Respond. Write down how God wants you to respond to today's Scripture reading and incorporate this learning into your life. Also, consider God's vision for the church and how you fit into the Body of Christ.

_____
_____
_____
_____
_____
_____
_____
_____
_____

DAY FIVE

Begin your sacred time with a few minutes of silence. Try to clear your mind and breathe deeply.

Read Acts 10:34-36 and listen God. Read the Scripture passage slowly two or three times. Write down thoughts or notes as God speaks to you. What words seem to jump off the page at you?

_____
_____
_____
_____
_____
_____
_____
_____
_____

Reflect on the ways that God has been with you recently and in your past, and give thanks to God. Rest in this daily practice. Try to build your time up to 15 minutes. Enjoy these quiet moments. You are cultivating deeper roots into the rhythm of your daily life.

_____
_____
_____
_____
_____
_____
_____
_____

Rest. Ask God to create in you a desire to know God in a deeper relationship.

Respond. Write down how God wants you to respond to today's Scripture reading and incorporate this learning into your life. Also, consider God's vision for the church and how you fit into the Body of Christ.

DAY SIX

Begin your sacred time with a few minutes of silence. Try to clear your mind and breathe deeply.

Read Acts 15:30-35 and listen for God. Read the Scripture passage slowly two or three times. Write down thoughts or notes as God speaks to you. What words seem to jump off the page at you?

Reflect on the ways that God has been with you recently and in your past, and give thanks to God. Rest in this daily practice. Try to build your time up to 15 minutes. Enjoy these quiet moments. You are cultivating deeper roots into the rhythm of your daily life.

_____
_____
_____
_____
_____
_____
_____
_____
_____
_____

Rest. Ask God to create in you a desire to know God in a deeper relationship.

Respond. Write down how God wants you to respond to today's Scripture reading and incorporate this learning into your life. Also, consider God's vision for the church and how you fit into the Body of Christ.

_____
_____
_____
_____
_____
_____
_____
_____
_____
_____

DAY SEVEN

Begin your sacred time with a few minutes of silence. Try to clear your mind and breathe deeply.

Read Acts 20:32-38 and listen for God. Read the Scripture passage slowly two or three times. Write down thoughts or notes as God speaks to you. What words seem to jump off the page at you?

_____
_____
_____
_____
_____
_____
_____
_____
_____
_____

Reflect on the ways that God has been with you recently and in your past, and give thanks to God. Rest in this daily practice. Try to build your time up to 15 minutes. Enjoy these quiet moments. You are cultivating deeper roots into the rhythm of your daily life.

_____
_____
_____
_____
_____
_____
_____
_____
_____

Rest. Ask God to create in you a desire to know God in a deeper relationship.

Respond. Write down how God wants you to respond to today's Scripture reading and incorporate this learning into your life. Also, consider God's vision for the church and how you fit into the Body of Christ.

_____

_____

_____

_____

_____

_____

_____

_____

_____

_____

_____

Notes

[1] *Raleigh News & Observer,* August 31, 2011:1-2D

[2] Martha Grace Reese, Unbinding the Gospel Project 2nd Report to the Lilly Endowment, 2010.

[3] Piet Levy, *Religion News Service,* October, 14, 2011.

[4] John Stott, *Through the Bible Through the Year,* Baker Books: Grand Rapids, 2006: 312.

CHAPTER FOUR

Formed by Prayer

"To be a Christian and to pray are one and the same thing; it is a matter that cannot be left to our caprice. It is a need, a kind of breathing necessary to life." — Karl Barth

I.

So far, you have been challenged to honestly examine your own desire for God. The image of a well-watered healthy tree has been our metaphor in order to emphasize the importance of a deep strong root system in our lives.

In the last chapter, we examined the ancient model for deep faith exemplified in the life of the early church in the Book of Acts. The nutrients of prayer, Scripture, worship, community, and missional service are clearly present in the fertile soil of this model for a life of deep faith. Now, it is time to focus on the sacred practice of prayer because prayer lies at the very center of communion with God. *How do you pray, and for what do you pray?*

Once upon a time, a young boy wanted a bicycle very badly. All his friends had one. Finally his mother suggested he take his concerns to the Holy Mother Mary in prayer. Johnny wrote his prayer out on a piece of paper before he went to bed, and prayed, "Mary, mother of God, could you see that I get a bicycle? All my friends have one. Amen." He placed the prayer next to his statue of the Virgin and went to sleep.

The next morning when he didn't have a bike, he wasn't discouraged. He repeated the same steps that night and every night for the next week, with the same disappointing result.

Finally he took his statue of Mary, wrapped it in a towel, and hid it in the back of a dresser drawer. When he went to sleep that night he prayed: "Jesus, if you want to see your mother again, I better get that bike!"[1]

Have you ever prayed like that? Do you think you really know how to pray? Be careful how you answer because St. Paul says that none of us really knows how we ought to pray. But fortunately, the Holy Spirit helps us speak.

In Romans 8:26-27, Paul writes: "The Spirit helps us in our weakness; for we do not know how to pray as we ought, but that very Spirit intercedes with sighs too deep for words. And God, who searches the heart, knows what is the mind of the Spirit, because the Spirit intercedes for the saints according to the will of God."

I'll admit that I don't know much about how to pray. I've read books on prayer, preached sermons on prayer, spent hours praying and leading prayer meetings, and prayer is still a mystery to me. The medieval German mystic, Meister Eckhardt, wrote: "If the only prayer you ever say in your entire life is 'thank you,' it will be enough." So maybe, "pray more, use fewer words" would be a good place for us to start when it comes to a discussion on prayer.

II.

Here in the second decade of the 21st century, our lives are busy and filled with worries. We are filled with fear about the future. Ironically, our usual response is to push God out of the way rather than invite God into the fray. The practice of prayer is to intentionally create space in our lives for God to have God's way.

Everything in our 24/7 culture constantly works against the practice of clearing out space for God to inhabit. We are always surrounded by noise from the radio, TV, iPod, Internet, traffic, children, etc. Many of us — myself included — even feel a bit of guilt if we're not doing something productive.

Yet we all need time for solitude, silence, reflection, meditation, and prayer. That's one thing I like about fall and winter. My internal clock urges me to get out for a few hours and sit in the woods in a deer stand, or to come home from work, build a fire, and settle in for the night. In the summer we crave time at the beach or a vacation in the mountains. It's all part of the seasonal rhythm of slowing down — recovery and renewal.

We tend to think that we are busier today than at any other time in history, but farmers and business owners of the past who had none of our modern conveniences would probably disagree. Even life in the first century was busy. For his final three years on earth, Jesus was a very busy person — from teaching, healing, and traveling to trouble-making. Yet Jesus practiced a prayer-filled life. It is clear from a reading of the Gospels that the central focus in Jesus' life was his relationship with God the Father.

Jesus said the he could do *nothing* apart from God the Father and that his entire mission was to do the will of God (John 5:19; Mark 14:32-36). Jesus frequently left the crowds and went to "a deserted place" to pray (Mark 1:35; 6:46; Matt. 14:22-23a; Luke 6:12).

Jesus was a role model for his disciples of the kind of intimacy with God that they should seek. That is why they said, "Lord, teach us to pray" (Luke 11:1). When we practice the prayer-filled life, we are moving into the same intimacy with God the Father that Jesus depended upon. The very nature of God as Father is love. God is the "waiting father" who runs to the end of the driveway every evening in hopes that his rebellious child will be coming home (Luke 15:11-32).

The disciples had watched Jesus pray with more focus and trust than anyone they had ever seen. Then they watched him perform miracles and heard him teach with unmatched power and wisdom. Soon they concluded that what Jesus said and did was connected to how he prayed. Next to Jesus, it was painfully obvious that these guys knew nothing about prayer.

In Luke's version of the Lord's Prayer, after Jesus had finished praying, one of his disciples finally blurts out: "Lord, teach us to pray!" Jesus modeled such an intimate relationship with his Father that at least one of the disciples dared to make this dangerous request. It is dangerous because the deeper we go with Jesus, the less our lives will ever be the same again. *Are you ready to begin such a journey toward a deeper faith?*

If we understand prayer as time spent cultivating our relationship with this kind of God, then we will want to go deeper; we will want to know God more. But how do we begin? This is the question that motivated the disciples to ask Jesus, "Lord, teach us to pray."

So if prayer is taught, then prayer is something that anyone can learn. I think prayer is also like air — something we know we must have in order to survive, yet we don't think consciously about every breath we take. To breathe is natural and for the Christian, to pray is natural.

Karl Barth said: "To be a Christian and to pray are one and the same thing; it is a matter that cannot be left to our caprice. It is a need, a kind of breathing necessary to life."[2] When the disciples said to Jesus, "Lord, teach us to pray" the model he gave them was this:

"Our Father which art in heaven, Hallowed be thy name.
Thy kingdom come, Thy will be done in earth, as it is in heaven.
Give us this day our daily bread. And forgive us our debts, as
we forgive our debtors. And lead us not into temptation, but

deliver us from evil. For thine is the kingdom, and the power, and the glory, for ever. Amen." (Matthew 6:9-13 KJV)

As early as 110-120 AD, a collection of the Apostle's teachings known as the *Didache* mentions that the Lord's Prayer was to be said three times daily by the earliest Christians. So the tradition of saying the Lord's Prayer was clearly in place as a part of the daily practice of living out one's faith in Christ. The act of saying this prayer is meant to lead the one saying it to a life embodying the very prayer in daily life.

It has been said that we don't choose the Lord's Prayer; it chooses us. As we submit ourselves to a life of deep faith, we learn to be people who are truthful. What we discover is that truth is not a set of propositions about the world; rather, truth is Jesus Christ. And we know this person by learning to pray as he taught us.

We ought to memorize this prayer and repeat it again and again. But learning to live this prayer and allowing it to become second nature to us takes time. In church we generally do most of the same things over and over again, week after week — telling the same stories and singing the same songs. Some complain that this makes church boring. But in worship, as in prayer, it is an intentional act of bending our lives toward God, and it is something we must learn to do over and over again — a holy habit.

When the disciples asked Jesus to teach them to pray, he didn't ask them, "Well guys, what do you think prayer is all about?" He said to them, "Pray like this. 'Our Father, who art in heaven . . .'"

So the Lord's Prayer is a gift to us from Jesus the Master Teacher. This is the *Lord's* Prayer. This prayer is not for getting what we want but rather for bending our wants toward what God wants. This is the Lord's Prayer, which means that this prayer teaches us to pray in the life and spirit of Jesus.

We should also understand that the Lord's Prayer becomes a lifelong act of bending our lives toward God in the way that God desires — "thy will be done, thy kingdom come." It is more about "bending" than "believing."

Finally, we need to realize that the Lord's Prayer is to be understood as "the prayer of a disciple," because it can only truly be prayed by the one who has entered into the lifelong journey of following after Jesus. Before we enter into the prayer itself, note the order of the petitions. The first three petitions have to do with God and the glory of God:

1) Our Father, which art in heaven,
2) hallowed (holy) by thy name.
3) Thy kingdom come, Thy will be done, in earth as is in heaven.

The second three petitions have to do with our needs and necessities:

4) Give us this day our daily bread
5) And forgive us our debts as we forgive our debtors,
6) And lead us not into temptation, but deliver us from evil . . .

So first, God is given God's supreme place, and only then can we turn to our own needs and desires. By remembering the order of the prayer and keeping it in proper order, we are always being reminded *that true prayer is not an attempt to bend the will of God to our desires but rather to submit our will to the will of God.*[3]

III.

Along with the disciples, we also know very little about prayer — if we're honest. Prayer is a mystery, and Jesus did not try to explain it away. What Jesus did was model a life of communion with God, and in so doing clearly demonstrate the necessity of prayer in the life of his followers.

So how do you define prayer? What does it mean for you to pray? And what do you need to learn about prayer? Mark 1:35 tells us: "In the morning, while it was still very dark, he (Jesus) got up and went out to a deserted place, and there he prayed."

Jesus modeled for us a life of prayer. Jesus also gave us a concrete model of how to pray. Jesus often prayed before he healed and gave thanks before he broke bread. He also went to pray in solitude away from his disciples.

Do you currently have a pattern or routine for daily prayer? Do you prayer in the morning after you brush your teeth? Do you pray at noon? Do you pray before bedtime? Or do you pray mainly before tests or when someone in your family gets sick? Is prayer a last resort for you, and a means of getting what you want — like the little boy who prayed for a new bike?

To pray is to change. The beginning and ending of all prayer is "the act of submitting my will to God's will." In between, there are many different kinds of prayers and many different ways in which to pray. But at the most basic level, to pray is to change. As we open ourselves to the will of and purposes of God, communion with God changes us.

We are always learning more about how to pray. So here are some examples of different ways that you can encounter God through the sacred practice of prayer:

Listening Prayer — Being still and silent before God is perhaps counterintuitive for many of us. Just try it. Ask nothing. Say nothing. Just listen. (See Psalm; 25:4-5; 27:14; 31:24; 37:7; 46:10-11)

Wordless Prayer — Perhaps our purest prayers occur when we have no idea what to pray and then the Holy Spirit takes over and utters prayers that are too deep for words (see Romans 8:26-27).

Spontaneous Prayer — Whenever someone or some circumstance comes into your mind, simply offer that person or circumstance over to God. Pray what is in your heart. Anytime. Anywhere. This is one aspect of how we "pray without ceasing" (see 1 Thessalonians 5:17) throughout the ordinariness of daily life.

Breath Prayer — This form of prayer can be practiced in sitting meditation or in the course of daily activities. As you breathe, open yourself to God's Spirit moving through your life, and experience the Spirit's centering, calming power renewing your whole being. Imagine that Jesus is breathing in and through you as he did with the disciples that first Easter (John 20:22).

Confessional Prayer — We are all sinners in need of God's forgiveness and grace. We need to ask God to cleanse us from known and unknown sin. The ancient church fathers and mothers would pray over and over throughout the day a prayer that has come to be known simply as the Jesus Prayer: "Lord Jesus Christ, Son of God, have mercy on me a sinner." (See also Psalm 51:10.)

Intercessory Prayer — This is the kind of prayer where we lift up others and their particular needs or circumstances before God (see Philippians 4:6-7 and 1 Corinthians 3:9). You may choose to make a list of those persons and concern that you want to offer to God in prayer.

Corporate Prayer — Besides our individual private prayer, we need to pray in the company of other disciples of Jesus. There is a divine power available "when two or three are gathered in my name," Jesus said in Matthew 18:19-20. The early Christians regularly devoted themselves to praying together (see Acts 1:14; 2:42; 4:31; 6:2-6; 16:16; 20:36). This is where the church connects with the power of God's Holy Spirit, and it cannot be underestimated!

Persistent Prayer — Don't stop praying! Don't give up. Jesus said, "Ask, seek, knock . . ." We are to "pray without ceasing . . ." (1 Thessalonians 5:17).

Scripture Prayer — *Lectio divina* is a Latin phrase meaning divine or sacred reading. *Lectio divina* provides us with a way to intertwine prayer with the Scriptures. It is a way of praying that dates back to many of the early followers of Jesus. There are many beautiful prayers already contained within the pages of Scripture. Furthermore, reading Scripture slowly and contemplatively enables us to offer the Word of God back to God. Then we allow God to speak to us through the words of Scripture. A simplified version of *lectio divina* is as follows:

   a. **Read.** (*lectio*) Select a short passage of Scripture and before reading take a few moments of silence. Now read slowly through the passage once allowing it to simply well up within you. Spend another moment in silence.
   b. **Reflect.** (*meditatio*) Read the passage a second time and reflect upon how these words touch your life today. *What do I need to hear in this passage? Is there a word or phrase that jumps out at me?*
   c. **Respond.** (*oratorio*) Read the passage for a third time and listen for how the word or phrases may be speaking to where you are in your life right now. Listen for what God is calling for in your life through the Scripture. Now you are ready to pour out your heart in response to God's word. Let the Scripture draw out your honest emotion. Write down how God wants you to respond to what you have heard.
   d. **Rest.** (*contemplatio*) Now simply rest in God's word and in God's acceptance and grace. Submit your will to God's will and delight yourself in the Lord.
   e. **Resolve.** (*incarnatio*) As a result of your encounter with God through praying the Scripture, resolve now to act upon the word that God has given you. Throughout the day remind yourself of this experience of God's presence, and continue your resolve to go deeper in faithful obedience to God's word.[4]

Thanksgiving Prayer — "Give thanks in all circumstances; for this is the will of God in Christ Jesus for you" (1 Thessalonians 5:17-18). God is good . . . all the time! No exceptions! God is able to make something good out of every life situation even though we cannot see it. It is a matter of trust.

"Thank you Jesus" is a good and simple prayer that bears repeating all through the day (Philippians 4:6-7).

Honest Prayer — Let's never make prayer a fake and insincere show of faith with God. Always be honest with God. God already knows what you need. God wants us to pray with honesty and humility. Let's make prayer real!

The most important lesson about prayer is not about *how* we pray, but *that* we pray! *Keep your focus on the person, not the process!* Prayer is more than communication with God — talking and listening. Prayer is a mysterious and deep *communion* with God that cannot be reduced to a formula. Feel the grace and freedom to try different approaches to prayer. Adapt a daily and weekly routine or "rule of life" that fits the life stage you happen to be in right now.

When I was single in my early twenties, I had hours each day that I could choose to spend in prayer and reading that I simply do not have at this stage in my life. Married with full-time jobs and living with children who have lots of extra-curricular activities makes solitude a challenge! But that's okay. Life will change again. Still, busyness is no excuse for not taking time to pray! Martin Luther reportedly used to say, "I have so much to do that I shall spend the first three hours in prayer."

In a few years I will be an "empty nester" trying to reinvent my daily and weekly routine and waiting for those checks in the mail from my highly successful adult sons! A retired widow has a very different life situation than a young mother of preschoolers. *So always remember that the goal and object of prayer is communion with God.*

In the verses that precede the "Lord's Prayer" in Matthew 6:5-8, Jesus gave a stern warning about prayer — not if you pray, but *when* you pray.

> "And whenever you pray, do not be like the hypocrites; for they love to stand and pray in the synagogues and at the street corners, so that they may be seen by others. Truly I tell you, they have received their reward. But whenever you pray, go into your room and shut the door and pray to your Father who is

in secret; and your Father who sees in secret will reward you. When you are praying, do not heap up empty phrases as the Gentiles do; for they think that they will be heard because of their many words. Do not be like them, for your Father knows what you need before you ask him."

So, if your Father already knows what you need before you ask him, why pray? The answer is so that you will commune with God and submit your will to God's will. Prayer changes us! So be creative, intentional, and above all, just pray!

The Psalmist wrote: "As a deer longs for flowing streams, so my soul longs for you, O God. My soul thirsts for the Living God" (Psalm 42:1-2a). That's the type of desire for God that Jesus wants us to have, and we can only find our true nourishment in prayer. Prayer is the first and most basic nutrient that we must intentionally cultivate deep into the soil of our lives in order for deep roots of faith to grow.

Heavenly Father,
To know you is to pray . . .
to love you is to pray . . .
to serve you is to pray . . .
to follow you is to pray.
Grant that I might learn to pray without ceasing with thanksgiving so that my life may become a prayer lived unto you each day,
in the name of Jesus Christ our Lord, who lives and reigns with you and the Holy Spirit,
one God, forever and ever. AMEN.

Consider the following prayer exercises as you begin cultivating a deep life of prayer. Be creative and don't allow yourself to design a rigid system of rules. Instead, experiment with daily, weekly, seasonal, and annual practices of prayer and solitude. Let the practice of prayer become joyful and life-giving!

1) Set aside five to ten minutes for prayer each morning and evening.

2) Spend five to ten minutes a day in silence. Hide in the bathroom if you must!

3) Read selections from a devotional book classic or book of prayers.

4) Pray the same short prayer throughout each day. "Lord Jesus Christ, Son of God, have mercy on me, a sinner" (The Jesus Prayer). "Create in me a clean heart, O God" (Psalm 51:10). I call this prayer statement my Trinity Prayer: "Father, Son, Holy Spirit." By simply saying these words, or breathing them silently, I feel a connection with God the Trinity.

5) Design your own daily journal based on the outline of "The Next Seven Days."

6) Practice the art of listening to God. Meditate on a Scripture verse paying attention to what God wants to tell you. Pay attention to the words and phrases that stand out to you.

7) Write a prayer in your own words in your daily journal.

8) Set aside an hour free from distractions once a week.

9) Learn to appreciate God through creation:

- Pray as you walk, jog, swim, play golf (yes, even between shots);
- Meditate and pray as you sit in a deer stand;
- Simply go outside look into the starry night sky.

10) Set aside ten minutes a week for thanksgiving.

11) Pray for the leaders in your church.

12) Get into the habit of offering "flash prayers." When you see someone, silently pray for that person. When a situation or need comes to mind, silently turn it over to God.

13) Try going to sleep praying and waking up praying. Don't feel guilty about falling asleep!

14) Listen to the Scriptures on your iPod as a way of entering into *lectio divina*.

15) Imagine God as always present with you wherever you are — even when you are unaware of God's presence.[5]

THE NEXT SEVEN DAYS

WEEK 4: Formed by Prayer

Over the next seven days continue to commit yourself toward the practice of making a sacred spiritual space in your daily routine in order to read the assigned Scripture, honestly reflect over your life, and pray.

Lectio divina is a Latin phrase meaning divine, or sacred, reading. *Lectio divina* provides us with a way to intertwine prayer with the Scriptures. It is a way of praying that dates back to early followers of Jesus. There are many beautiful prayers already contained within the pages of Scripture. Furthermore, reading Scripture slowly and contemplatively enables us to offer the Word of God back to God. Then we allow God to speak to us through the words of Scripture. A simplified version of *lectio divina* is as follows.*

1) **Read.** (*lectio*) Select a short passage of Scripture. Before reading take a few moments of silence. Now read slowly through the passage one time allowing it to simply well up within you. Spend another moment in silence.

2) **Reflect.** (*meditatio*) Read the passage a second time reflecting upon how these words touch your life today. *What do I need to hear in this passage? Is there a word or phrase that jumps out at me?*

3) **Respond.** (*oratorio*) Read the passage a third time listening for how the word or phrases may be speaking to where you are in your life right now. Listen to what God is calling for in your life through the Scripture. Now you are ready to pour out your heart in response to God's word. Let the Scripture draw out your honest emotion and write down how God wants you to respond to what you have heard.

4) **Rest.** (*contemplatio*) Now simply rest in God's word and in God's acceptance and grace. Submit your will to God's will and delight yourself in the Lord.

5) **Resolve.** (*incarnatio*) As a result of your encounter with God through praying the Scripture, resolve now to act upon the word that God has given you. Throughout the day remind yourself of this experience of God's presence and continue your resolve to go deeper in faithful obedience to God's word.

*adapted from Barton, Ruth Haley. *Sacred Rhythms: Arranging Our Lives for Spiritual Transformation.* Downers Grove, IL: InterVarsity Press, 2006: 54-61.

DAY ONE

Begin your sacred time with a few minutes of silence. Try to clear your mind and breathe deeply.

Read Jeremiah 29:11-14a and listen for God. Using the process of *lectio divina*, read through the Scripture passage slowly three or four times. Write down thoughts, words, or phrases as God speaks to you.

_____
_____
_____
_____
_____
_____
_____
_____
_____

Reflect on the ways that God has been with you recently and in your past, and give thanks to God. Enjoy these quiet moments.

_____
_____
_____
_____
_____
_____
_____
_____
_____

Rest at the end of praying the Scripture. You are cultivating deeper roots into the rhythm of your daily life.

Respond by asking God to create in you a desire to know God in a deeper relationship of prayer. Write down a short prayer to God for this day.

_____
_____
_____
_____
_____
_____
_____
_____
_____
_____

DAY TWO

Begin your sacred time with a few minutes of silence. Try to clear your mind and breathe deeply.

Read Matthew 7:7-11 and listen for God. Using the process of *lectio divina*, read through the Scripture passage slowly three or four times. Write down thoughts, words, or phrases as God speaks to you.

_____
_____
_____
_____
_____
_____
_____
_____
_____

Reflect on the ways that God has been with you recently and in your past, and give thanks to God. Enjoy these quiet moments.

Rest at the end of praying the Scripture. You are cultivating deeper roots into the rhythm of your daily life.

Respond by asking God to create in you a desire to know God in a deeper relationship of prayer. Write down a short prayer to God for this day.

DAY THREE

Begin your sacred time with a few minutes of silence. Try to clear your mind and breathe deeply.

Read Psalm 46:10-11 and listen for God. Using the process of *lectio divina*, read through the Scripture passage slowly three or four times. Write down thoughts, words, or phrases as God speaks to you.

_____
_____
_____
_____
_____
_____
_____
_____
_____
_____

Reflect on the ways that God has been with you recently and in your past, and give thanks to God. Enjoy these quiet moments.

_____
_____
_____
_____
_____
_____
_____
_____
_____

Rest at the end of praying the Scripture. You are cultivating deeper roots into the rhythm of your daily life.

Respond by asking God to create in you a desire to know God in a deeper relationship of prayer. Write down a short prayer to God for this day.

_____
_____
_____
_____
_____
_____
_____
_____
_____
_____

DAY FOUR

Begin your sacred time with a few minutes of silence. Try to clear your mind and breathe deeply.

Read 1 Thessalonians 5:17-18 and listen for God. Using the process of *lectio divina*, read through the Scripture passage slowly three or four times. Write down thoughts, words, or phrases as God speaks to you.

_____
_____
_____
_____
_____
_____
_____
_____

Reflect on the ways that God has been with you recently and in your past, and give thanks to God. Enjoy these quiet moments.

_____
_____
_____
_____
_____
_____
_____
_____
_____
_____
_____
_____

Rest at the end of praying the Scripture. You are cultivating deeper roots into the rhythm of your daily life.

Respond by asking God to create in you a desire to know God in a deeper relationship of prayer. Write down a short prayer to God for this day.

_____
_____
_____
_____
_____
_____
_____
_____
_____
_____
_____
_____

DAY FIVE

Begin your sacred time with a few minutes of silence. Try to clear your mind and breathe deeply.

Read Philippians 4:6-7 and listen for God. Using the process of *lectio divina*, read through the Scripture passage slowly three or four times. Write down thoughts, words, or phrases as God speaks to you.

_____
_____
_____
_____
_____
_____
_____
_____
_____
_____

Reflect on the ways that God has been with you recently and in your past, and give thanks to God. Enjoy these quiet moments.

_____
_____
_____
_____
_____
_____
_____
_____
_____
_____

Rest at the end of praying the Scripture. You are cultivating deeper roots into the rhythm of your daily life.

Respond by asking God to create in you a desire to know God in a deeper relationship of prayer. Write down a short prayer to God for this day.

_____
_____
_____
_____
_____
_____
_____
_____
_____

DAY SIX

Begin your sacred time with a few minutes of silence. Try to clear your mind and breathe deeply.

Read Matthew 6:5-8 and listen for God. Using the process of *lectio divina*, read through the Scripture passage slowly three or four times. Write down thoughts, words, or phrases as God speaks to you.

_____
_____
_____
_____
_____
_____
_____
_____
_____

Reflect on the ways that God has been with you recently and in your past, and give thanks to God. Enjoy these quiet moments.

_____
_____
_____
_____
_____
_____
_____
_____
_____
_____

Rest at the end of praying the Scripture. You are cultivating deeper roots into the rhythm of your daily life.

Respond by asking God to create in you a desire to know God in a deeper relationship of prayer. Write down a short prayer to God for this day.

_____
_____
_____
_____
_____
_____
_____
_____
_____
_____

DAY SEVEN

Begin your sacred time with a few minutes of silence. Try to clear your mind and breathe deeply.

Read Matthew 6:9-13 and listen for God. Using the process of *lectio divina*, read through the Scripture passage slowly three or four times. Write down thoughts, words, or phrases as God speaks to you.

_____
_____
_____
_____
_____
_____
_____
_____
_____
_____

Reflect on the ways that God has been with you recently and in your past, and give thanks to God. Enjoy these quiet moments.

_____
_____
_____
_____
_____
_____
_____
_____
_____

Rest at the end of praying the Scripture. You are cultivating deeper roots into the rhythm of your daily life.

Respond by asking God to create in you a desire to know God in a deeper relationship of prayer. Write down a short prayer to God for this day.

_____
_____
_____
_____
_____
_____
_____
_____
_____
_____

Notes

[1] Dan Shutters, "Laugh Lines," *Presbyterians Today*, December 1997: 3.
[2] Karl Barth, *Prayer*. The Westminster Press: Philadelphia, 1949: 35-36.
[3] William Barclay, *Matthew*. Philadelphia: The Westminster Press, 1975: 199.
[4] Ruth Haley Barton, *Sacred Rhythms: Arranging Our Lives for Spiritual Transformation*. Downers Grove, IL: InterVarsity Press, 2006: 54-61.
[5] Adapted and enlarged from *A Spiritual Formation Workbook*, by James Bryan Smith with Lynda Graybeal. HarperSanFrancisco, 1999: 32-36.

CHAPTER FIVE

Formed by Scripture

"All Scripture is inspired by God and useful for teaching, for reproof, for correction, and for training in righteousness, so that everyone who belongs to God may be proficient, equipped for every good work."
— 2 Timothy 3:16-17

I.

So far I have challenged you to honestly examine your individual desire for God. We have looked at the image of a well-watered healthy tree to emphasize the importance of a deep, strong roots system in our lives. We have examined the ancient model for *deep faith* exemplified in the life of the early Church in the Book of Acts where the nutrients of prayer, Scripture, worship, community, and missional service were clearly present in the soil of their life together.

In the last chapter we focused on the most basic nutrient of *prayer* that must be present in the soil of deep faith. The early Church was certainly a people of prayer. The next clearly definable practice in the deep faith of the early Church was their *devotion to the apostles teaching*. They were a learning church that loved to dig into the rich soil of Holy Scripture.

The events of Acts 2 took place during the annual Jewish harvest festival, or Festival of Weeks (Shavuot), which commemorated God giving the Ten Commandments at Mount Sinai fifty days after the Exodus. The celebration was called Pentecost (Greek for fiftieth). What happened on Pentecost Day as recorded in Acts 2 was truly amazing. The Holy Spirit came upon them and God began teaching the people through the Apostles whom Jesus had previously anointed and trained. There were more than 3,000 new converts that day. As a result, the Holy Spirit opened up a huge class of instruction for these new believers, and the Apostles were the teachers.

For all we know, the details about Jesus — who he was, what he said and did, how he died and rose from the dead — were truly new information for these 3,000 people. They had come from all over the world. They were starting from scratch in the Jesus Movement so they needed instruction.

Throughout the Book of Acts, Luke uses the Greek word *mathetai* in describing the Christ-followers of the Church. The word means disciples, learners, or pupils. And there was a lot to learn for these new followers of Jesus. Much was at stake for the success of this new movement with Jesus now gone from their midst. But even though these new converts had been mystically and powerfully moved by God at Pentecost, they did not get a free pass to stop using their minds. Their *emotional* experience with God's Spirit did not negate their intellect.

On the contrary, they were compelled to embrace *learning* and receiving instruction from the Apostles. So from the earliest days of the church, it is clear that God wants Christians to use their minds and exercise their intellect as disciples of Jesus. In fact, this is part of fulfilling the Great Commandment — to love God with your heart, soul, *mind*, and strength (Mark 12:29-31).

Simply put, we cannot disengage our minds and love God fully! To put it another way, to be full of God's spirit and to be anti-intellectual are mutually incompatible! Jesus referred to the Holy Spirit as the "Spirit of truth." So wherever God's spirit is present, truth matters.

For those early Christians, learning their new faith was so crucial that Luke, the author of Acts, puts it first in his list — and we should take notice. The learning dimension of cultivating deep faith is just as important today is it was in the first-century.

For Christians, the Holy Spirit is ultimately our teacher, but the Holy Spirit also chooses to use human teachers. The early Christians were eager to learn all they could about Jesus and the coming kingdom of God. They knew that Jesus had chosen and appointed the apostles, so they willingly submitted to the apostle's authority. *But that did not mean they were to let the Apostles do their thinking for them!*

II.

Further along in the Book of Acts, the Apostle Paul commended the Jews of Beroea for being "more receptive than those in Thessalonica, for they welcomed the message very eagerly and examined the Scriptures every day to see whether these things were so" (17:11).

These people were eager to hear Paul preach, but they didn't blindly assume that he knew everything he was talking about! They weren't looking for a shortcut to faith, e.g., "you find the truth, preacher, and then hand it over to us." The Beroean seekers were excited about doing their own digging and discovery, and they didn't mind a little dirt and sweat in the process.

People of deep faith have a radical passion for digging into God's Word and letting the truth set them free! The word *radical* comes from the Latin word "*radix*" which means root, such as in "radish." This is what it means to be a follower of Jesus–*to be one who gets at the root, or the truth, of things*. But to get to the root you must dig — through dirt and soil, worms and rocks, and a wide array of modern-day trash. You will get dirty, and it will require some real work on your part. But it is possible to sift through this muck until you finally discover the root.

Several years ago, Robert Fulghum wrote a popular book called, *All I Really Need to Know I Learned in Kindergarten*.[1] It was filled with lots of great advice such as: hold hands when crossing the street, don't hit people, take a nap every afternoon, share everything, and always flush the toilet! And you have to admit that the world would be a better place if we all just followed this simple advice. But of course, life is not lived forever in Kindergarten. Kindergarten is crucial to our formation academically and socially just as being schooled in Holy Scripture is crucial to our formation spiritually.

Sadly, many Christians have never grown out of the flawed philosophy of "come to church every once and awhile, hear a Bible story, go home, and get back to your life unchanged." One of the greatest myths that is buried deep within the soil of American Christianity today is that we are supposed to get to a certain point in life and stay there, comfortable and secure, because change is unnatural and thus to be avoided at all costs! Remember our lesson on prayer? To pray is to change!

We short-circuit the very nature of faith itself — to grow and learn and become — if we are only interested in reaching a certain point and settling down. The invitation Jesus gave to people was "follow me." This implies motion and movement.

Again, the word "disciple" means "pupil or learner." This word is used some 248 times in the four gospels and 22 times in the Book of Acts! This is what Jesus had in mind for us — an active, living, growing relationship — not some passive, self-serving existence.

Jesus was most often called *Rabbi* or Teacher, thus if we are to be his disciples then we must behave like his students or learners. The clear implication is that we are to think, we are to ask questions, we are to listen, we are to pay attention, we are to learn, and we are to act.

We dive deep into our faith with all our heart, soul, *mind*, and strength. The person who follows Jesus has a life-long curiosity as one who asks, seeks, knocks, and digs deep in Holy Scripture.

III.

The modern reality for North America is that biblical illiteracy abounds. We cannot assume that people know what we're talking about when we mention Jesus and the Bible. Once upon a time, Americans may have been people of the Book, but that is no longer the case. In fact, the chances are very great that your children and grandchildren will know less about the Bible and ways of Jesus than you do — unless we recommit ourselves toward cultivating the vital nutrient of Scripture into the soil of our lives.

A nationwide poll conducted in 2010 by the Pew Center Forum on Religion and Public Life U.S. produced some interesting data about our religious knowledge. For example:

- Nearly six-in-ten U.S. adults say that religion is "very important" in their lives, and roughly four-in-ten say they attend worship services at least once a week.
- 71 percent know that, according to the Bible, Jesus was born in Bethlehem.
- 63 percent correctly name Genesis as the first book of the Bible.
- A little more than half know that the Golden Rule — "Do unto others as you would have them do unto you" — is *not* one of the Ten Commandments.
- 45 percent can name all four Gospels (Matthew, Mark, Luke and John).
- 37 percent say they read the Bible or other Holy Scriptures at least once a week, but Americans as a whole are much less inclined to read other books about religion.
- Of the three Old Testament figures asked about in the survey, Americans are most familiar with Moses. 72 percent know he was the biblical figure who led the exodus.
- Abraham is less well known, with 60 percent identifying him as the biblical figure who was willing to sacrifice his son's life for God.
- 39 percent identify Job as the biblical figure known for remaining obedient to God despite extraordinary suffering.

The data indicates that educational attainment is the single best predictor of religious knowledge. Other factors include reading Scripture at least once a week and talking about religion with friends and family. Those who say that they attend worship services at least once a week generally demonstrate higher levels of religious knowledge than those with medium or low religious commitment.

And people *outside the South* score better than Southerners. The oldest group in the population (age 65 and older) actually gets fewer questions right than other age groups. However, people 65 and older do about as well as people under age 50 on questions about the Bible and Christianity. They simply do less well on questions about other world religions. You can go to pewforum.org to view the complete report.

Ironically, in the twenty-first century there are an incredible number of new aids for Bible study — computer and multi-media based resources and apps for your Smartphone. There are more tools available for the student of the Bible than at any other time in the history of the church.

Just think about how many copies of the Bible you have in your home! Access to Scripture obviously does not necessarily equate to biblical knowledge, much less transformation. Although the Bible is more accessible to us than at any other time in history and there are dozens of translations and sizes and covers and styles, reading the Bible is neither ubiquitous nor easy.

It has been reported that one of the most widely-known Bible verses among adults and teens, including those who go to church, is: "God helps those who help themselves" — which isn't in the Bible and is actually contrary to the basic message of grace clearly revealed in the New Testament!

A cartoon in The New Yorker portrayed a man inquiring at the counter of a large bookstore. The clerk, peering into her computer screen, says, "The Bible? Let's see, that would be in the 'Self Help' section."

The cartoon sarcastically points out one of the challenges we face in reading the Bible as Christians in consumer-driven North America. The Bible has largely become just one more consumer option, one more source of therapeutic advice alongside books on dieting, dating, astrology, and other strategies for successful people.

As a result, we lose what the Bible offers us — not "self help," but rather help we cannot provide for ourselves at all! The Bible is a book about God, God's creation, human sin, rebellion, and the real possibility for redemption, forgiveness, and a new creation. We cannot help ourselves.

Another challenge in reading Scripture is the unfortunate reality that there are always some people who seem to know exactly what the Bible means for all of us. Some say the Bible is always to be taken literally. As a result, Scripture may be used to support discrimination, violence, or oppression of certain groups of people.

For example, during the 19th century, by using certain Bible verses as proof texts, slavery was defended as divinely ordained and permissible. Unfortunately, the cultural and religious story of our own experience often becomes the lens through which we see the Bible's story.

If someone ever claims you must take the Bible literally — word for word — or not all, then ask him if you should take John the Baptist literally when he calls Jesus the Lamb of God. Or if you have to take Jesus literally when he says, "if your eye causes you to sin then gouge it out" and "if your arm causes you to sin then cut it off."

Reading *and* understanding the Bible can be a challenge. One of our problems is the tendency to stress contemporary experience as the sole judge and source of our thinking about God. We often place great value on our personal, contemporary experience — isolated from the flow of history.

"Contemporary experience" then tends to take over the authority of the Bible. Our thinking begins to sound this way: "If it works, it must mean that God is blessing it, therefore, it is biblical."

But God's Word wants to do more than merely speak to our contemporary experience and modern dilemmas. The Bible judges, reforms, guides, and enriches our lives. Scripture offers us experiences of God that we would not have had without digging into the Bible for ourselves. The words of Scripture should be meditated upon, memorized, interpreted, and then instilled into our lives in order to counter the advice that the world tells us is true.

The Bible is our great gift from God. It is the most important book ever written. It is full of instruction and knowledge. Yet the central purpose of approaching Scripture is not primarily for information, but for *transformation*. The Psalmist wrote: "Your word is a lamp unto my feet and a light unto my path" (Psalm 119:105). Holy Scripture illuminates the way in which God's people are to live. It reveals God's will and ways to us. So, how are we to read Scripture as God's Word for today? I want to offer eight brief guidelines, or suggestions:

1) **Read Holy Scripture as Authoritative.** Because we believe that the original and definitive witness to God's saving action are preserved in

the texts of the Bible, we must be a community that treasures and respects the written word. We are not free to make other texts authoritative — even good and helpful ones — until we submit to the authority of Scripture. This requires us to cultivate disciplines of attentive reading and listening and memorizing. *God's Word has authority over your life!*

2) **Read Scripture in Community.** We should read the text together with our sisters and brothers in the faith who may challenge and enrich our individual reading. The Bible was not written *only* to be taken home and read in private. Others in the church hold us accountable for not only faithful interpretation, but also faithful living of the word of Scripture. *Scripture calls us into a corporate obedience as the church.*

3) **Read Scripture in its Historical Context.** To bridge the gap between the ancient setting of the text and our modern situation, we should seek to discover who wrote the passage, when it was written, where the writing took place, and what the historical circumstances were. Knowing something of the historical background is essential to good interpretation. We need to understand that the Scripture was written for a specific people in a specific time. So we need to ask ourselves questions like: *What did the author likely intend for the original audience? How is this biblical text asking me to change? How does my world blind me to the message that this text is attempting to get me to hear and apply?*

4) **Read Scripture Theologically.** We must remember that the Bible's main purpose is to convey principles and truths about God. Therefore, the reader of the Bible is concerned with letting those theological truths emerge from the text rather than bringing our own preconceived ideas to the passage. God Word is about God — written from faith for faith!

5) **Read the Whole Context of Scripture.** The Bible is more than a collection of spiritual sound bites. There is a wholeness to the story it tells — a story that runs from Genesis to Revelation, from creation to final redemption of the world. Even though we read much Scripture in our churches, we often read just a few sentences at a time, just a bit from this book of the Bible, then a bit from that book. But when we look for the larger perspective, we also become more aware of the individual voices in the Bible. *For instance, Luke's*

portrait of Jesus has features that distinguish it from John's portrait. So taking the whole Bible in its larger context helps avoid proof texting, i.e., picking out isolated verses here and there that support some favorite doctrine or issue while avoiding other verses that might speak a different word about that particular issue.

6) **Read the Scripture as Israel's Story.** The Old Testament and New Testament together constitute the Christian Bible. Therefore, we are not free as Christians to ignore the testimony of Israel. The God whom Jesus proclaimed is the God of Abraham, Isaac, and Jacob (Mark 12:26), and we understand our identity as God's children only if we know ourselves as "Abraham's offspring, heirs according to the promise" (Galatians 3:29).

7) **Read the Scripture as the Church's Story.** While the Bible is inspired by God, it did not just drop down upon us from on high in an Old English leather-bound edition! The Bible has been transmitted to us through the testimony of generations of wise and faithful followers. So Scripture reading in the church depends on our capacity to read the Bible in conversation with the past while in conversation with the history of interpretation of these texts in the Church. In other words, we don't read the Bible alone in our time and place. We read in communion with the saints, which saves us from being held captive to our own age and culture.

8) **Read Scripture as Your Story.** Once we determine what the text meant *then,* we must next decide what it means *now.* When we read or hear the Bible, we need to ask ourselves, *So what? What difference does it make?* And then we ask: *Now what? What is God's word for me in this passage, and what does God want me to do with it?*

As James says:

> But be doers of the word, and not merely hearers who deceive themselves. For if any are hearers of the word and not doers, they are like those who look at themselves in a mirror; for they look at themselves and, on going away, immediately forget what they were like. But those who look into the perfect law, the law of liberty, and persevere, being not hearers who forget but doers who act — they will be blessed in their doing. (James 1:22-25)

IV.

Think of these guidelines as you encounter Scripture. If you're not engaging yourself in God's Word on a regular basis, then start with a simple plan and become a part of a Bible study group.

Being formed by Scripture doesn't take a degree in theology — it just requires some intentional desire and commitment toward learning. It can happen at home in front of an open Bible, reading a few verses or a chapter a day. It can happen in a Sunday School Class or a small group in the company of other disciples of Jesus. Here are a few practical suggestions for how to get started in your own reading of Scripture:

- Read through one of the four gospels (Matthew, Mark, Luke, or John) using a highlighter to underline words and verses that speak to you.
- Take a small book of the Bible such as James or Philippians, and read it through. Keep a journal for taking notes.
- Use a Bible commentary to assist you in doing a verse-by-verse study of a section of Scripture.
- Spend an entire month reading and re-reading the Sermon on the Mount (Matthew 5-7).
- Read through the entire Bible in one year.
- Read a Proverb or Psalm each day.
- Memorize a verse of Scripture each week or month.
- Use "The Next Seven Days" at the end of each chapter of this book as a model for beginning to read, reflect, rest, and respond to Holy Scripture. Get a blank notebook and make it personal.

Is it really possible for us to devote ourselves to the Apostle's teaching since there are no more Apostles alive today who have their same authority? We do it by submitting to their teachings as revealed in the New Testament. It is within the pages of Scripture that we have the teaching and authority of the Apostles handed down to us. The two primary issues we should be honest with are: 1) our lack of a hunger for God's word, and 2) our lack of time to devote in learning God's word.

Honestly, we all make time for the things that most important to us. What we are largely missing is a true desire to know God and an intentional commitment toward making *learning* a priority for our personal faith and the faith of our children. We need to admit that the reason we don't make time to learn God's word personally and corporately is that it's not very important to us. God's Word is a mirror so we have to be willing to be honest as open ourselves to it. Hebrews 4:12-13 says,

> Indeed, the word of God is living and active, sharper than any two-edged sword, piercing until it divides soul from spirit, joints from marrow; it is able to judge the thoughts and intentions of the heart. And before him no creature is hidden, but all are naked and laid bare to the eyes of the one to whom we must render an account.

Ouch! Scripture is always the best commentary on Scripture! The Bible takes honesty, humility, time, patience, perseverance, and courage to read. It is a part of the process of spiritual formation that happens over time as we arrange our lives around spiritual practices that help us grow deeper in our faith.

Not even the Apostles who walked with Jesus were formed into the image of Christ overnight. It took lots of time and teaching, trials and tribulations to remold and remake them into the image of their Rabbi and Lord.

In 2 Corinthians 3:18, Paul says we are being "transformed" into the likeness of Christ. He uses the Greek word *metamorphoumetha* — metamorphosis.

When my sons were young, during the summer months they would often find big, fat, juicy caterpillars in our backyard. What they couldn't see on the surface was that the caterpillar was undergoing a *metamorphosis* — a change that would result in its transformation from a slimy, slow crawling caterpillar into a majestic butterfly that would one day flap its glorious wings and take flight.

The caterpillar does not become a butterfly in an instant. The process of transformation takes time. And in the same way, we need to be patient as we engage Scripture. We must understand that our goal is nothing less than to be transformed into the image of Christ and a lifestyle that reflects his ways.

Scripture may seem difficult to understand at times — and not just because the Bible is ancient and written from cultures different than ours. The Bible is also difficult because it is God's Word to us, a word that sometimes afflicts our comforts in addition to comforting our afflictions! Frederick Buechner puts it this way:

> If you look at a window, you see specks, dust, the crack where Junior's baseball hit it. But if you look through a window, you see the world beyond. Something like this is the difference between those who see the Bible as an irrelevant bore, and those who see it as the Word of God which speaks out of the depths of an almost unimaginable past into the depths of ourselves.[2]

Scripture opens our eyes and our possibilities to the world beyond. As St. Paul says to Timothy: "All Scripture is inspired by God and useful for teaching, for reproof, for correction, and for training in righteousness, so that everyone who belongs to God may be proficient, equipped for every good work" (2 Timothy 3:16-17).

When you are finished with this *Deep Faith* study, I urge you to make a commitment to continue in God's Word. Create your own notebook or spiritual journal and a plan that fits you. You don't have to spend an hour a day reading the Bible. Just do something! Read Scripture. Meditate upon it. Listen to it. Apply it. Cultivate the gift of Scripture — God's Word for us — into the soil of your life!

Gracious God,
Your words are a light unto our path;
like a compass, they guide me and point me in the way I should go.
Help me desire your Word more and more, and to take our delight in its teachings for my life.
Thank you for your wonderful words of life, through Jesus Christ the Living Word, by the breath of the Holy Spirit. AMEN.

THE NEXT SEVEN DAYS

WEEK 5: Formed by Scripture

Over the next seven days, continue to commit yourself toward the practice of making a sacred spiritual space in your daily routine in order to read the assigned Scripture, honestly reflect over your life, and pray.

DAY ONE

Begin your sacred time with a few minutes of silence. Try to clear your mind and breathe deeply.

Read Matthew 7:24-29 and listen for God. Go through the process of *lectio divina*. Read the Scripture passage slowly three or four times. Write down thoughts, words, or phrases as God speaks to you.

_____
_____
_____
_____
_____
_____
_____
_____

Reflect on God's being with you recently and in your past. Give thanks to God. Rest and respond at the end of praying the Scripture. Enjoy these quiet moments — cultivating deeper roots into the rhythm of your daily life.

_____
_____
_____
_____
_____
_____
_____

Rest. Ask God to create in you a desire to know God and God's word in a deeper way.

Respond. Meditate over what God's word means to you and how God's word has spoken to you today. What application do you sense God's wants you to make in your life?

_____
_____
_____
_____
_____
_____
_____
_____
_____

DAY TWO

Begin your sacred time with a few minutes of silence. Try to clear your mind and breathe deeply.

Read Acts 17:10-13 and listen for God. Go through the process of *lectio divina*. Read the Scripture passage slowly three or four times. Write down thoughts, words, or phrases as God speaks to you.

_____
_____
_____
_____
_____
_____
_____
_____

Reflect on the ways that God has been with you recently and in your past, and give thanks to God. Rest and respond at the end of praying the Scripture. Enjoy these quiet moments. You are cultivating deeper roots into the rhythm of your daily life.

_____
_____
_____
_____
_____
_____
_____
_____
_____
_____

Rest. Ask God to create in you a desire to know God and God's word in a deeper way.

Respond. Meditate over what God's word means to you and how God's word has spoken to you today. What application do you sense God's wants you to make in your life?

_____
_____
_____
_____
_____
_____
_____
_____
_____
_____

DAY THREE

Begin your sacred time with a few minutes of silence. Try to clear your mind and breathe deeply.

Read Hebrews 4:12 and listen for God. Try going through the process of *lectio divina*. Read through the Scripture passage slowly three or four times. Write down thoughts, words, or phrases as God speaks to you.

_____
_____
_____
_____
_____
_____
_____
_____
_____
_____

Reflect on the ways that God has been with you recently and in your past, and give thanks to God. Rest and respond at the end of praying the Scripture. Enjoy these quiet moments. You are cultivating deeper roots into the rhythm of your daily life.

_____
_____
_____
_____
_____
_____
_____
_____
_____
_____

Rest. Ask God to create in you a desire to know God and God's word in a deeper way.

Respond. Meditate over what God's word means to you and how God's word has spoken to you today. What application do you sense God's wants you to make in your life?

_____

_____

_____

_____

_____

_____

_____

_____

_____

DAY FOUR

Begin your sacred time with a few minutes of silence. Try to clear your mind and breathe deeply.

Read 2 Timothy 3:16-17 and listen for God. Try going through the process of *lectio divina*. Read through the Scripture passage slowly three or four times. Write down thoughts, words, or phrases as God speaks to you.

_____

_____

_____

_____

_____

_____

_____

Reflect on the ways that God has been with you recently and in your past, and give thanks to God. Rest and respond at the end of praying the Scripture. Enjoy these quiet moments. You are cultivating deeper roots into the rhythm of your daily life.

_____
_____
_____
_____
_____
_____
_____
_____
_____

Rest. Ask God to create in you a desire to know God and God's word in a deeper way.

Respond. Meditate over what God's word means to you and how God's word has spoken to you today. What application do you sense God's wants you to make in your life?

_____
_____
_____
_____
_____
_____
_____
_____
_____
_____

DAY FIVE

Begin your sacred time with a few minutes of silence. Try to clear your mind and breathe deeply.

Read Psalm 119:1-2 and listen for God. Try going through the process of *lectio divina*. Read through the Scripture passage slowly three or four times. Write down thoughts, words, or phrases as God speaks to you. What seems to jump off the page at you?

_____

_____

_____

_____

_____

_____

_____

_____

_____

Reflect on the ways that God has been with you recently and in your past, and give thanks to God. Rest and respond at the end of praying the Scripture. Enjoy these quiet moments. You are cultivating deeper roots into the rhythm of your daily life.

_____

_____

_____

_____

_____

_____

_____

_____

_____

Rest. Ask God to create in you a desire to know God and God's word in a deeper way.

Respond. Meditate over what God's word means to you and how God's word has spoken to you today. What application do you sense God's wants you to make in your life?

_____
_____
_____
_____
_____
_____
_____
_____
_____

DAY SIX

Begin your sacred time with a few minutes of silence. Try to clear your mind and breathe deeply.

Read Psalm 119:11 and listen for God. Try going through the process of *lectio divina*. Read through the Scripture passage slowly three or four times. Write down thoughts, words, or phrases as God speaks to you.

_____
_____
_____
_____
_____
_____
_____
_____

Reflect on the ways that God has been with you recently and in your past, and give thanks to God. Rest and respond at the end of praying the Scripture. Enjoy these quiet moments. You are cultivating deeper roots into the rhythm of your daily life.

_____
_____
_____
_____
_____
_____
_____
_____
_____
_____

Rest. Ask God to create in you a desire to know God and God's word in a deeper way.

Respond. Meditate over what God's word means to you and how God's word has spoken to you today. What application do you sense God's wants you to make in your life?

_____
_____
_____
_____
_____
_____
_____
_____
_____
_____

DAY SEVEN

Begin your sacred time with a few minutes of silence. Try to clear your mind and breathe deeply.

Read Psalm 119:105 and listen for God. Try going through the process of *lectio divina*. Read through the Scripture passage slowly three or four times. Write down thoughts, words, or phrases as God speaks to you. What seems to jump off the page at you?

_____

_____

_____

_____

_____

_____

_____

_____

Reflect on the ways that God has been with you recently and in your past, and give thanks to God. Rest and respond at the end of praying the Scripture. Enjoy these quiet moments. You are cultivating deeper roots into the rhythm of your daily life.

_____

_____

_____

_____

_____

_____

_____

_____

Rest. Ask God to create in you a desire to know God and God's word in a deeper way.

Respond. Meditate over what God's word means to you and how God's word has spoken to you today. What application do you sense God's wants you to make in your life?

_____
_____
_____
_____
_____
_____
_____
_____
_____
_____

Notes

[1] Robert Fulghum, *All I Really Need to Know I Learned in Kindergarten*. New York: The Random House Publishing Group, 1986.

[2] Frederick Buechner, *Wishful Thinking*. San Francisco: HarperSanFrancisco: 12.

CHAPTER SIX

Formed by Worship and Community

I.

Worship and community — they go together. These two nutrients are absolutely essential in order for deep roots of faith to grow. Of course, worship is an opportunity we have before us every day as individuals. You can worship God alone while driving in your car listening to music, or being outdoors in God's amazing creation. You can also worship with other followers of Jesus on Sundays or in small groups during the week. Worshiping alone and worshiping in community can both become something we take for granted. So there are some basic questions we probably should ask ourselves about worship and community, such as:

Why do we worship? *How* are we to worship? *What* do you expect from worship? What does *God* expect from our worship? Do we really need to worship *together*? While we may provide many different answers to these questions, one thing is clear — *worship lies at the heart of Christian faith and at the very core of the nature of the church.*

The worship of God takes many forms and styles in the Bible, just as it does across the world today. Sometimes the congregation is small, and the preacher is a layperson; sometimes the congregation numbers in the thousands, and the music is accompanied by an orchestra; sometimes the worshipers are in jeans and shorts as they sing to the driving beat of electric guitars and drums; sometimes the congregation is silent and contemplative.

Yet no matter the size, style, or culture of a congregation, worship is meant to be at the center of our life together as the church and as individual Christians. It was certainly at the center of the life of the early Christians. Acts 2:46 tells us that day by day, "they spent much time in the temple, they broke bread together in homes and they also ate food with generous hearts, praising God . . . ."

The phrase in 2:42, "they devoted themselves to the prayers," is likely an allusion to prayer services or prayer meetings. Worship and community was not just an opportunity that came once a week on Sunday mornings for the early Christians. They gathered often for support and prayer, worship and teaching.

New Testament worship is a *daily lifestyle experience* as we continually engage the presence of God in our vocation, family and community life. Paul says in Romans 12:1: "I appeal to you therefore, brothers and sisters, by the mercies of God, to present your bodies as a living sacrifice, holy and acceptable to God, which is your spiritual worship."

New Testament worship is a corporate experience as we gather together in the unity of the Holy Spirit as a group, and this transcends our individualism. This is our true strength as we draw nourishment from our worship and community.

New Testament worship is a *Trinitarian experience* because we are worshiping God as Father, Son, and Holy Spirit. It is a mystery that takes place when we worship, but our worship is distinctively focused on the Trinitarian nature of the God we know and experience in *threeness* yet perfect oneness.

New Testament worship is finally culminated in the worshiper's *response of obedient service* to the God whom we worship as we serve others in the world that God has created. Worship, in the biblical sense, is a lifestyle of devotion to God the Father, Son, and Spirit which is lived out personally and within the community of faith.

II.

A few decades ago when Eastern Europe was firmly in the grip of communism, the kinds of activities we take for granted in our Western churches such as youth camps, social programs, and education, were completely forbidden. The Rev. Leonid Kishkovsky told the U.S. Conference of the World Council of Churches this startling news: "Those who created these rules were convinced that if churches were deprived of everything but worship, if all they could do was pray to a God who didn't exist, then they would wither and die." Since they didn't, he added: "American Christians are challenged to understand that it is in worship that the church finds the energy for all of its life and work."[1]

When Christians gather together, there should life and energy in our worship of God! In fact, if our passion and hunger for the authentic worship of God is not growing, then we cannot grow deep in any other area of church life. That's just how important worship is to the individual Christian and to the gathered church!

The 19th century Danish theologian Søren Kierkegaard tells the parable of a community of ducks waddling off to duck church to hear the duck preacher. The duck preacher spoke eloquently of how God had given the ducks wings with which to fly. With these wings there was nowhere the ducks could not go; there was no God-given task the ducks could not accomplish. With these wings they could soar into the presence of God himself. Shouts of "amen" were quacked throughout the duck congregation. At the conclusion of the service, the ducks left, commenting on what a wonderful message they had heard — and then they waddled all the way back home.

Too often, we worshipers waddle away from worship just as we waddled in — unchanged and afraid to use the wings which God has gifted us with in order to fly. Maybe it's because we are creatures of habit. Week after week we sit in the same place in the same pew, following a familiar order of service, and listening to a sermon that we assume is intended for someone else.

Kierkegaard also suggested that we understand worship as a *drama* where God — not the congregation — is the audience, where the preacher and worship leaders serve as the prompters, and the congregation comprises the cast of actors.

Now, this is a radically different approach from our modern "consumer mentality" where the worshiper is viewed as the consumer of a product that the church and its leaders must market and package in a way that meets that consumer's felt needs. If the consumer is not satisfied with the product, then the consumer will simply move on to a place that might better "meet his or her needs" — or serve better coffee.

The biblical truth is that experiencing God through worship has more to do with our inner attitudes and motives of the heart than with the performances of those designated as "worship leaders." *It is a personal matter and a corporate matter!* And if Kierkegaard is right, worship is meant to be more of a "participatory sport" than a "spectator sport!"

In his book, *Celebration of Discipline*, Richard Foster defines worship as "the human response to the divine initiative." It is God who seeks, draws, and persuades his children to come to him. Worship is kindled within us only when the Spirit of God touches our human spirit — Spirit touching spirit.

As a result, we should not be overly concerned with questions about the correct form or style for worship. Singing and praying, praising and silence, chanting and liturgy, pipe organs and praise bands may all lead to worship, but worship happens when our spirit is ignited by our Creator.

When God's Spirit touches our own spirit, the issue of styles and forms are secondary — not irrelevant or unimportant, but definitely secondary. The object of our worship is God and God alone.[2]

Jesus said in John 4:23-24: "But the hour is coming, and is now here, when the true worshiper will worship the Father in spirit and truth, for the Father seeks such as these to worship him. God is spirit, and those who worship him must worship in spirit and in truth." I want to suggest three nutrients that should be present in the soil of our worship if we are to worship God in spirit and in truth.

III.

The first nutrient needed in the soil of our worship is an understanding of who God is and of who we are.

In worship, we recognize that *God* has created us, and God has redeemed us. He is God and we are not. Psalm 100 says: "Know that the Lord is God. It is he that made us and we are his; we are his people and the sheep of his pasture" (v.3). Paul writes, "You are not your own, you are bought with a price" — through the blood of Christ.

In worship, we recognize God's rightful place. God is not the proverbial "man upstairs." In worship we come into the presence of a holy God, the Creator and Redeemer, the One without beginning or end. The writer of Hebrews calls us "to offer to God an acceptable worship with reverence and awe; for indeed our God is a consuming fire" (12:28-29). When God's spirit touches our spirit then we are consumed by the God whom we worship. We cannot walk away unaffected and unchanged. Think about those times in Scripture when people experienced the awesome reality of God:

- Moses had to take his shoes off because he was on holy ground. Job was brought to say, "My ears had heard of you, but now my eyes have seen you."
- Isaiah said, "I am ruined: My eyes have seen the King, the Lord Almighty."

- As Isaiah worshiped in the Temple and saw the Lord, he said, "Woe is me! I am ruined! For I am a man of unclean lips . . ." Then the seraph flew over to him, touched his lips . . . and pronounced that his guilt was taken away. (Isaiah 6:1-8)
- When Thomas saw the resurrected Jesus he proclaimed, "My Lord and my God."
- And when John sees the Christ in the first chapter of Revelation he says, "I fell at his feet as though dead."

To worship God, we begin by recognizing what kind of God it is we worship. We recognize God's holiness and claim on our lives. Then we recognize our true human condition.

A second nutrient needed in the soil of our worship is a realization of our need for one another.

We all come as people in need of doing something with our sin and guilt and hurt. One fact that we seldom acknowledge on a Sunday morning is that everybody in the pews is hurting. We all come as sinners in need of God's touch of grace. So we come together hoping in some way to reach up to God but believing in faith that God will reach down to us.

In John Steinbeck's novel, *The Grapes of Wrath*, he deals with the masses of displaced people moving west during the Great Depression. In it he writes: "And because they were lonely and perplexed, because they had all come from a place of sadness and worry and defeat, and because they were all going to a new mysterious place, they huddled together."[3]

There is often something similar taking place when we come to worship. We all face difficult choices and circumstances in an uncertain world, so we come and huddle together. We do not worship alone. We worship in community with God's people. We need one another, and when we come together we are assured that Jesus is present just as he said, "where two or three are gathered in my name, there I am with them."

The mighty redwood trees of California's Sequoia National Park are the largest life-forms on Earth. The great Sequoia trees tower as much as 300 feet above the ground. I've seen a picture of a Redwood so large that a car can drive through the cut out in the base of its trunk. Surprisingly, these giant trees have very shallow root systems that reach out in all directions to capture the greatest amount of surface moisture. Seldom will you see a redwood standing alone, because high winds would quickly uproot it. That's why they grow in clusters. Their intertwining roots provide support for one another. The storms that blow their way through the valleys of the Sierra Nevada can do no harm to those trees because they stand strong and tall together . . . *in community.*

A third nutrient needed in the soil of our worship is a desire to be obedient to God.

At the end of a typical worship service, many congregations traditionally sing a hymn as an invitation for our response to God. There are good biblical reasons for that. Isaiah didn't just recognize God in worship, he responded to God with, "Here I am, send me." James and John and Matthew and the rest of the disciples didn't just listen to Jesus, they responded by following him.

Jesus always called people to a radical and public response to his preaching of the Good News. Thus we need to take seriously the fact that God expects a response when we worship him. Worship first requires a response to God's offer of salvation. But next it involves a response to God's challenge for us to do something with our lives and follow Christ in a lifetime of discipleship.

Abraham Lincoln is said to have gone to church with a friend one Sunday. Afterwards the friend asked, "What did you think of the preacher?" Lincoln replied, "He was tall and a good speaker." This was not exactly the answer his friend was looking for, so he asked, "Did you like the preacher?" Lincoln said, "No," because he honestly did not. "And why not?" asked the friend. Lincoln replied, "Because he did not ask us to do anything great for God."[4]

In my vocation, I have to remind myself that preaching is not about how polished of a preaching performance I give or how many compliments I hope to receive. *It's about challenging the church to do something significant for God!* Maybe the great thing for you to do would be to teach a class, invite a friend to church, tutor a child, or help serve in the community without anyone twisting your arm. Genuine worship demands a response from every worshiper, and God expects that we come open and ready to be changed. *The world waits to be touched by those whose spirit has been touched by God's spirit.*

A fourth nutrient needed in the soil of our worship is transformation.

As with prayer, worship should change us. And this is something that God does. We shouldn't be the same people going out as we were coming in. That's what genuine worship does to people. A true encounter with God sends us off in a new direction. Worship fills us, lifts us up, equips us, and gives us strength that will sustain our faith for the times that lie ahead.

If God's spirit has touched our spirit, if we truly worship God, then we will *re-form* our lives. We will leave the sanctuary with new hopes, new dreams, and new desires to soar into God's future. In other words, we won't waddle out as we waddled in! In her book, *Teaching a Stone to Talk*, Annie Dillard paints a potent picture of what it is like to underestimate the power of transforming worship. She writes:

> Why do people in churches seem like cheerful, brainless tourists on a packaged tour of the Absolute . . . Does anyone have the foggiest idea what sort of power we so blithely evoke? Or, as I suspect, does no one believe a word of it? The churches are children playing on the floor with their chemistry sets, mixing up batches of TNT to kill a Sunday morning. It is madness to wear ladies' straw hats and velvet hats to church; we should all be wearing crash helmets. Ushers should issue life preservers and signal flares; they should lash us to our pews. For the sleeping God may wake someday and take offense, or the waking god may draw us out to where we can never return.[5]

Maybe we *should* attach a warning label at the top of our worship bulletins! Because when you have truly worshiped the God of the universe, your life will be *transformed* — and that is something God does regardless of the style, the size, or the volume of our worship service.

IV.

Two more things are worth mentioning about the worship and community of the early church and how their example of *worship and community* should inform our vision today.

First, their worship was both formal and informal. They worshiped in the temple and in their homes. We know they continued to attend the traditional prayer services in the temple, which were somewhat formal, and we know they supplemented these with their own distinctively Christian worship gatherings celebrating the Eucharist in their homes. So the early church had elements that were both liturgical and spontaneous, structured and unstructured, formal and informal — and so should we.

Second, the early church's worship was both joyful and reverent. Acts 2:46 says the gathered community had joyous (generous) hearts. One of the fruits of the spirit is joy, and sometimes we need to be reminded to loosen up and let in a little more uninhibited joy! Worship is serious business, but it's not all doom and gloom. At the same time, the early church's worship was never irreverent or trite. Joy and reverence go together to make for authentic worship in spirit and truth.[6]

For the early Christians gathered in worship the resulting impact was that "awe came upon everyone" because there was a mixture of both wonder and humility as the people experienced God in worship day after day. The early Christian community emphasized corporate worship — gathering together as a group and gathering with a unity of spirit that transcended their individualism (Acts 2:42-47, Hebrews 10:25, Philippians 3:15). Joyfully *and* reverently, God wants us to be a worshiping community of disciples.

Isaac Pennington said that when God's people gather for worship they are like "a heap of fresh and burning coals warming one another as a great strength and freshness and vigor of life flows through into all."[7] If you take away a glowing piece of coal from the cluster, it will eventually burn itself out if left on its own. That's just how essential our life together as a community of disciples is in relation to our own individual faith.

V.

At our best moments — when we get past ourselves to share the worship of God with others — we are given a little taste of heaven on earth in this experience of sharing. It is discovered in the Greek word *koinonia*, which has to do with the basic idea of fellowship, and sharing community. *Koinonia* is found in Acts 2:42: "They devoted themselves to the apostles and teaching and fellowship (koinonia), to the breaking of bread and prayers."

Koinonia is what defines our "life together" as the body of Christ. *Koinonia* is the experience of distinctively *Christian* fellowship between very human people in the setting of the church. This *koinonia* is something that simply cannot be found anywhere else.

Don't get me wrong — as a Christian you can and must be deeply involved in community organizations, school activities, clubs, and service groups. That is what Jesus means when he says, "You are the salt of the earth . . . the light of the world," and we must be *in* the world in order to be salt and light.

However, no matter how meaningful these groups might become for you, not one of them *can* or should replace the need for being in community with other Christ-followers. No matter how many problems or hypocrites you see in the church, the gathered body of believers is what Jesus Christ established, and it will remain until he comes again.

That is not to say that churches won't become irrelevant and die, because they will if they are not open to new ways and forms of the Spirit for new and challenging times. But God will always have the Church in the world because the *Church is people*, and the Church exists because it is God who has constituted the Church.

First John 1:3,6 tells us that: "Our koinonia is with the Father . . . If we say we have koinonia with him while we are walking in darkness, we lie and do not do what is true, but if we walk in the light as himself is in the light, we have koinonia with one another and the blood of Jesus his Son cleanses us from all sin."

So there is the *koinonia* we share "with Christ." This is what we are called to — a relationship of fellowship with Jesus himself (1 Corinthinans 1:9). We experience the living example of this fellowship, or communion, through the Lord's Supper in our worship together.

There is also the *koinonia* "in the Spirit" we share together (2 Corinthinans13:13; Phillippians 2:1). As Christians, we live together in the shared presence of the Holy Spirit, and we are to function with the help and guidance of the Spirit of God.

So we share in a *koinonia* that is Trinitarian — we participate in fellowship with the Father, Son, and Holy Spirit. There are plenty of things that separate us such as age, gender, nationality, politics, college loyalties, etc. But we are united in the fact that Christians worship the same triune God, the same Lord.

We also experience *koinonia* outwardly through a "practical sharing" with those who are less fortunate. This is the word Paul uses to refer to the collection he was organizing among the Greek churches to be distributed among the poverty-stricken churches in Judea. Paul uses the word three times in connection with the collection he took from the churches for the poor at Jerusalem (Rom. 15:26; Cor. 8:4, 9:14). Christian *koinonia* always expresses itself outwardly in ways of practical giving to others.

Koinonia is the bond which binds Christians to each other, to Christ, to the Spirit, and to God the Father. Nothing happens to us alone because we are all bound together by this *koinonia* in the church. Further, we can't truly grow closer to one another unless we are drawing closer to God. In his book, *The Pursuit of God*, A.W. Tozer raises this point:

> Has it ever occurred to you that one hundred pianos all tuned to the same (tuning) fork are automatically tuned to each other? They are of one accord by being tuned — not to each other — but to another standard to which each one must individually bow.[8]

So, the implication is that a hundred worshipers gathered looking away from themselves and to Christ are more united than they could possibly be if they were to turn their eyes away from God and focus on fellowship with one another. In other words, we grow closer to one another as we tune our hearts and lives to God in worship!

This is what we must remember as we share life and worship together in the imperfect church. God has come down to us in the person of Jesus and laid down his life on a cross; therefore, we must always come down to each other and love just he loved us. This is the essence of the grace that God shares with us and that we are called to share with one another. We discover both through worship and community — essential nutrients in the soil of *deep faith*.

Holy God,

You alone are worthy to be praised; you alone are worthy to be worshiped. Help us approach you — individually and collectively — with a sincere spirit, honestly seeking after truth, and open to being transformed by the living Lord Jesus Christ through the power of the Holy Spirit. AMEN.

THE NEXT SEVEN DAYS

WEEK 6: Formed by Worship & Community

Over the next seven days, continue to commit yourself toward the practice of making a sacred spiritual space in your daily routine in order to read the assigned Scripture, honestly reflect over your life, and pray.

DAY ONE

Begin your sacred time with a few minutes of silence. Try to clear your mind and breathe deeply.

Read John 4:23-24 and listen for God. Using the process of *lectio divina*, read the Scripture passage slowly three or four times. Write down thoughts, words, or phrases as God speaks to you.

_____
_____
_____
_____
_____
_____
_____
_____
_____

Reflect on the ways that God has been with you, and give thanks.

_____
_____
_____
_____
_____
_____
_____
_____
_____

Rest. Ask God to create in you a desire to know God and God's word in a deeper way.

Respond. Consider one or two concrete ways that you can worship God more faithfully *and* build a deeper sense of community with other Christians. You are cultivating deeper roots into your daily life.

_____
_____
_____
_____
_____
_____
_____
_____
_____

DAY TWO

Begin your sacred time with a few minutes of silence. Try to clear your mind and breathe deeply.

Read Romans 12:1-2 and listen for God. Using the process of *lectio divina*, read through the Scripture passage slowly three or four times. Write down thoughts, words, or phrases as God speaks to you.

_____
_____
_____
_____
_____
_____
_____

Reflect on the ways that God has been with you, and give thanks.

_____
_____
_____
_____
_____
_____
_____
_____
_____
_____

Rest. Ask God to create in you a desire to know God and God's word in a deeper way.

Respond. Consider one or two concrete ways that you can worship God more faithfully *and* build a deeper sense of community with other Christians. You are cultivating deeper roots into your daily life.

_____
_____
_____
_____
_____
_____
_____
_____
_____
_____

DAY THREE

Begin your sacred time with a few minutes of silence. Try to clear your mind and breathe deeply.

Read Hebrews 10:24-25 and listen for God. Using the process of *lectio divina*, read through the Scripture passage slowly three or four times. Write down thoughts, words, or phrases as God speaks to you.

_____

_____

_____

_____

_____

_____

_____

_____

_____

Reflect on the ways that God has been with you, and give thanks.

_____

_____

_____

_____

_____

_____

_____

_____

_____

Rest. Ask God to create in you a desire to know God and God's word in a deeper way.

Respond. Consider one or two concrete ways that you can worship God more faithfully AND build a deeper sense of community with other Christians. You are cultivating deeper roots into your daily life.

DAY FOUR

Begin your sacred time with a few minutes of silence. Try to clear your mind and breathe deeply.

Read Hebrews 12:28-29 and listen for God. Using the process of *lectio divina*, read through the Scripture passage slowly three or four times. Write down thoughts, words, or phrases as God speaks to you.

Reflect on the ways that God has been with you, and give thanks.

_____
_____
_____
_____
_____
_____
_____
_____
_____
_____

Rest. Ask God to create in you a desire to know God and God's word in a deeper way.

Respond. Consider one or two concrete ways that you can worship God more faithfully AND build a deeper sense of community with other Christians. You are cultivating deeper roots into your daily life.

_____
_____
_____
_____
_____
_____
_____
_____
_____
_____
_____

DAY FIVE

Begin your sacred time with a few minutes of silence. Try to clear your mind and breathe deeply.

Read Matthew 14:32-33 and listen for God. Using the process of *lectio divina*, read through the Scripture passage slowly three or four times. Write down thoughts, words, or phrases as God speaks to you. What seems to jump off the page at you?

_____

_____

_____

_____

_____

_____

_____

_____

_____

Reflect on the ways that God has been with you, and give thanks.

_____

_____

_____

_____

_____

_____

_____

_____

_____

Rest. Ask God to create in you a desire to know God and God's word in a deeper way.

Respond. Consider one or two concrete ways that you can worship God more faithfully AND build a deeper sense of community with other Christians. You are cultivating deeper roots into your daily life.

_____
_____
_____
_____
_____
_____
_____
_____

DAY SIX

Begin your sacred time with a few minutes of silence. Try to clear your mind and breathe deeply.

Read Psalm 105:2-4 and listen for God. Using the process of *lectio divina*, read through the Scripture passage slowly three or four times. Write down thoughts, words, or phrases as God speaks to you. What seems to jump off the page at you?

_____
_____
_____
_____
_____
_____
_____
_____

Reflect on the ways that God has been with you, and give thanks.

_____
_____
_____
_____
_____
_____
_____
_____
_____
_____
_____
_____

Rest. Ask God to create in you a desire to know God and God's word in a deeper way.

Respond. Consider one or two concrete ways that you can worship God more faithfully AND build a deeper sense of community with other Christians. You are cultivating deeper roots into your daily life.

_____
_____
_____
_____
_____
_____
_____
_____
_____
_____

DAY SEVEN

Begin your sacred time with a few minutes of silence. Try to clear your mind and breathe deeply.

Read Colossians 3:16 and listen for God. Using the process of *lectio divina*, read through the Scripture passage slowly three or four times. Write down thoughts, words, or phrases as God speaks to you. What seems to jump off the page at you?

_____
_____
_____
_____
_____
_____
_____
_____

Reflect on the ways that God has been with you, and give thanks.

_____
_____
_____
_____
_____
_____
_____
_____

Rest. Ask God to create in you a desire to know God and God's word in a deeper way.

Respond. Consider one or two concrete ways that you can worship God more faithfully AND build a deeper sense of community with other Christians. You are cultivating deeper roots into your daily life.

_____
_____
_____
_____
_____
_____
_____
_____
_____
_____
_____

Notes

[1] *Savannah News-Press*, Saturday, January 11, 1992 - 3C.

[2] Richard Foster, *Celebration of Discipline.* Harper & Row, San Francisco: 1988: 159.

[3] John Steinbeck, *The Grapes of Wrath.* New York: Penguin Group, 1939: 193.

[4] William Benton, *Where the Water Hits the Wheel.* Smyth & Helwys, 1993: 72.

[5] Annie Dillard, *Teaching a Stone to Talk.* New York: Harper, 1983: 40.

[6] John Stott, *Through the Bible through the Year*, Grand Rapids: Baker Books, 2006: 310.

[7] Marjorie J. Thompson, *Soulfeast: An Invitation to the Christian Spiritual Life*, Louisville: WJK, 1995: 56.

[8] A.W. Tozer, *The Pursuit of God*, Harrisburg, PA: Christian Publications, 1948: 97.

CHAPTER SEVEN

Formed by Missional Service

"Peace be with you. As the Father has sent me, so I send you."
— John 20:21

I.

When I first led the *Deep Faith* study in my own congregation, this final chapter on missional service happened to fall on the first Sunday in Advent. Finishing the study as Advent was beginning did not seem to be the best timing. But the more I thought about it, the more it made sense. God is a sending God. The Father has sent Jesus his son as the hope of our faith into the world. Just as God was incarnate in the flesh, Christ now sends us into the world to incarnate his love as God's missional people!

During this study we have been introduced to the *deep faith* model of the Jerusalem church in Acts chapter two. We have learned that the focal point in the Book of Acts is about the *community* of disciples the Holy Spirit was forming and shaping and how their relationships were at the core of the early church. We have explored the sacred spiritual practices of prayer, Scripture, worship, and community. *So far, these practices refer to life on the inside — to the church's interior life together.* They tell us virtually nothing about the church's outreach to the world.

If we stop at Acts 2:42 then the early church appears to be living for themselves — preoccupied with *Bible study, fellowship dinners, and worship* while ignoring the lonely and lost outside of their membership.

But that was not the case. The early Christians were also committed to God's sending mission in the coming of Christ, but it's not until verse 47 that we see it. Verse 47 teaches us three important lessons about the early church's outreach beyond themselves:

First, it was God who "added to their number," says verse 42. Of course, the Lord did this through the preaching of the apostles, the daily witness of church members, and their community of love and hospitality. But it was God who added to their number. Only God's Spirit can open the eyes of the spiritually blind, unplug the ears of the spiritually deaf, and give life to the spiritually dead. Only God can add people to the church and transform lives.

Second, God added to their number "those who were being saved." Notice God didn't add to their number without saving them, nor did he save them without adding them to the church. In other words, personal salvation and membership in the community of Christ's church do go together.

Third, God added to their number those who were being saved . . . "daily." The early Christians did not view evangelism and mission as occasional activities of the church. Every single day people were being added to the church. Clearly this is something that God does, but God chooses to use a loving community of Christians to accomplish God's mission.[1]

II.

So how does this take place today? The mission frontier of the twenty-first century has moved from the foreign field to local communities. The church of today now meets the world through the lives of its own members! This is absolutely crucial to understand if we are to re-orient ourselves — and our churches — for participating in God's mission in the world today.

Just think about some of the incredible changes that have come to our world in the past one hundred years! A hundred years ago, the average wage in the U.S. was 22 cents an hour; more than 95 percent of all births took place at home; the average life expectancy in the U.S. was 47 years; only 8 percent of homes had a telephone; there were only 8,000 cars in the U.S.; sugar cost 4 cents a pound; eggs were 14 cents a dozen; most women only washed their hair once a month; the five leading causes of death were: 1) pneumonia and influenza, 2) tuberculosis, 3) diarrhea, 4) heart disease, and 5) stroke; only 6 percent of all Americans had graduated high school.[2]

Some describe the age we are living today in as "post-Christian" — which would help explain why many of the old methods of outreach don't work anymore. The landscape has changed. It's a new era. Everything we do as individual Christians and as churches will be shaped by our basic understanding — or misunderstanding — of mission.

So, we must begin to see our identity being shaped primarily from a biblical sense of mission rather than from an old denominational or cultural sense of identity. We must become missional Christians and a "missional church" — moving from a people who occasionally do mission projects to a people who understand themselves as being on God's mission right where we live 24/7.

If we are really to understand the mission of the church, we must first understand the mission of God (*missio dei*). Beginning with Abraham, God intended to establish God's reign in all the earth through a people. Israel was to be that people — a missionary people, a light unto all other nations. Even when Israel as a whole refused God's mission, God did not abandon the idea that the reign — or the kingdom — of God must have a people. God's kingdom is revealed in and through the lives of God's people. That's how God has chosen it to be.

God's mission continued through the sending of his son Jesus Christ, and the community of disciples Jesus established, AKA "the church." So it is more accurate to say the Church doesn't have a mission, but rather the church participates in God's mission![3]

When we look at the early church's life together, we get a sense that they really understood their lives were to be lived out in missional service for others. The most radical characteristic of the early church was the elimination of all social distinctions and barriers because of the love and grace and forgiveness they found in Christ. For Jesus, above all else, the community that would come to be known as the church was a place for "sinners."

Then as the church put into action the love ethic of Jesus, they became a living demonstration of God's love for the world. And the Lord added to their number. It is really by our love that people will know that we are Christ's disciples. There is no shortcut to love. People see if we are genuine or not. Love costs. A deep sincere love must be interwoven through all the roots of faith if faith is to truly grow. Henri Nowen wrote:

> Love deeply. Do not hesitate to love and to love deeply. You might be afraid of the pain that deep love can cause. When those you love deeply reject you, leave you, or die, your heart will be broken. But that should not hold you back from loving deeply. The pain that comes from deep love makes your love

ever more fruitful. It is like a plow that breaks the ground to allow the seed to take root and grow into a strong plant.

> The more you have loved and have allowed yourself to suffer because of your love, the more you will be able to let your heart grow wider and deeper . . . Yes, as you love deeply, the ground of your heart will be broken more and more, but you will rejoice in the abundance of the fruit it will bear."[4]

To be caught up into God's mission is to love the world. In loving the world we will embody the gospel of Christ in the world, we will proclaim it to the world, we will enact it for the world, and we anticipate God's future kingdom when all things will be under the reign of Christ.[5]

III.

So, how are we supposed to enact God's mission? In Acts 1:8, Jesus tells his disciples just before he ascends to the Father: "You will be my witnesses in Jerusalem, and in all Judea and Samaria, and to the ends of the earth." When Jesus told this to his followers they were in Jerusalem. He was saying, first, you must start at home. Start with the people closest to you in your own city, your own community. Then go to Judea and Samaria — your surrounding regions. And ultimately he says, "You are to go to the ends of the earth."

Notice Jesus doesn't say, "You will be my defense attorney." You don't have to defend God. He doesn't say, "You will be my prosecutor." You don't need to be God's enforcer. Jesus didn't say, "You will be my salesman." You don't have to twist anybody's arm for God. All God asks you to do is be a *witness*.

A witness is someone who simply tells what they have seen and heard and experienced. Nobody can be a better witness of what God has done in your life than you, because you are the authority on your life — not your pastor, not your parents, not anybody else.

God is building a family of people from every nation, and the amazing part is that God has chosen us to participate in the mission. We are to serve God by serving others as missional Christians. *So, how do we get started?* Imagine concentric circles moving out from the center representing your life and influence in the world.

Begin by paying attention to those people in your immediate circle.

In Luke 8:39, after Jesus healed a man, the man wanted to travel with Jesus. Here's what Jesus said to him: "'Return to your home, and declare how much God has done for you.' So he went away proclaiming throughout the city how much Jesus had done for him." Your mission starts right at home — in your own neighborhood, in your own community. God wants you to go to your friends, your family, your coworkers, your neighbors, and those whom you already know.

Sometimes this is the hardest thing to do because people already know you. You can't fake it. And that's actually good news. You don't have to be perfect, but you do have to be honest. Missional service begins in your immediate circle of relationships.

Next, open your eyes and ears to those in your community.

God's love demands that we move beyond our comfort zones to serve people with different backgrounds, different ethnicities, different educational levels, different languages, and different economic levels. God's mission to the world means that we must be willing to take risks in order to share the message. The Apostle Paul said in 1 Corinthians 9:22: "I have become all things to all people, that I might by all means save some." In other words, I can't just hang out with people who are like me. Christ-followers are called to build bridges, not walls! Missional service moves us beyond our familiar relationships and out of our comfort zone.

Finally, you must care about the whole world.

We have to care about the whole world because God cares about the whole world. You may already know John 3:16: "For God so loved the world that he gave his only son . . ." You may also know the Great Commission in Matthew 28:19: "Go therefore, and make disciples of all nations, baptizing them in the name of the Father and of the Son and of the Holy Spirit, and teaching them to obey everything that I have commanded you."

Jesus was talking to all his followers. So, if you're a Christian, you are sent on mission to live in this world just as Jesus was sent on mission by his Father — just as the Word became flesh and dwelt among us.

When Jesus spoke the Great Commission to his disciples, they didn't have ability to crisscross continents. In those days, the primary means of transportation was to walk, ride a donkey, or take a small boat. Today, we have planes, ships, trains, cars, buses and, of course, the Internet. You can sit in your pajamas and communicate with people all over the world!

But to take it a step further, the world has come to us. America is a nation of immigrants. In my own county in North Carolina we have significant populations of Hispanic, Haitian, Asian, African and European peoples.

During the past few years in the small-town church where I serve, we have provided space on Sundays for Christians to worship in three languages — Spanish, Creole, and English! You simply cannot care about your immediate world without caring about the whole world, because the world is right here!

There are daily opportunities to pay attention to God's spirit and serve the people that cross our paths. You might call these "random acts of missional service."

There is also the necessity of being intentional with our service. For many of us, we need to plan ahead and schedule some "not so random acts of missional service" in order to keep this nutrient fresh and growing in the soil of our faith.

So, here are 20 simple ways to become more missional in your living:

1) Discover you spiritual gifts and then ask God to place you where you can best be used to serve.
2) Help out around the house without being asked.
3) Volunteer at a homeless shelter, soup kitchen, or prison ministry.
4) Do something anonymously for a neighbor or friend in need.
5) Visit the sick and shut-in.
6) Donate blood.
7) Volunteer one Saturday at a Habitat for Humanity work site.
8) Volunteer as a mentor or tutor at an after-school program.
9) Learn about an injustice and determine to act with compassion.
10) Start a recycling program for your church.
11) Learn about poverty, hunger, and immigration in your community and educate your church about how you can meet needs.
12) Write thank-you notes to people in your church and community who may serve without being noticed.
13) Participate on a mission trip outside of your community.
14) Be a regular at a local café or park so that you get to know the people in your community.

15) Walk or run around your neighborhood so you can meet people and see life from the street level.

16) Invite neighbors for a cookout.

17) Babysit for a young parent or sit with an elderly adult.

18) Start a missional community group in your home.

19) Volunteer to coach a little league or community sports team.

20) Get involved in your kids school as a mentor or PTA volunteer.

IV.

The book I referred to in chapter one, *Almost Christian: What the Faith of Our Teenagers Is Telling the American Church*, is based on the findings of the recent National Study of Youth and Religion Survey. Kendra Creasy Dean concludes in her book that our churches and parents must have "missional imaginations" that are willing to engage in the mission of God in our communities, not for the churches' gain, but to further the kingdom of God.[6]

She says the church is both the problem and the solution. The research data shows that when we present a weakened form of our faith that exalts "niceness" over engagement in justice issues, when we exclude people from our churches who are not like us, or when we present the "American Dream" as Christ's ideal for us, then we fail our youth. Instead, we need to embrace the mission of God and reorient our churches, inspiring our youth to follow Christ into the world to serve the poor and oppressed.[7] Until we commit to this vision of the church's mission, it's hard to blame our youth for thinking that "being nice" and following the status quo is the same as following Jesus.

The story is told of two rival Kentucky farmers who owned racing stables. One spring, each of them entered a horse into a local steeplechase race. Thinking that a professional rider might help him outdo his friend, one of the farmers hired a jockey. The two horses were neck and neck with a large lead over the rest of the pack at the last fence, when suddenly both riders fell.

The professional jockey remounted quickly and rode on to win the race. Afterward, the jockey found the farmer who had hired him fuming with rage. The jockey asked, "What's the matter? I won didn't I?" The farmer yelled, "You won all right, but you crossed the finish line on the wrong horse!"[8]

In all his hurry to remount, the jockey had jumped on the wrong horse! People do this all the time. Churches do this all the time. We settle for something easy or more convenient than the horse we have been called to ride upon. We get busy doing things that we assume are important and necessary — and they may well be. Yet these things may be a different horse than the one we have been given to ride. Whatever success we achieve in life is meaningless if we're on the wrong horse. Being connected to God's mission for our lives and his church is the only horse worth riding on.

Emil Brunner said, "As a fire exists by burning, the church exists by mission."[9] There are a lot of good things that you as an individual (and churches) can be involved with today that are not central to God's mission. Success as individuals and as churches cannot be measured by winning or climbing to the top, but rather by being faithful to God's mission.

God's mission in the world today is taking place in and through the lives of those who are the Church — the body of Christ. As the Father has sent the Son, the Son has sent the people of God in the power of the Holy Spirit that the world might believe. Missional service is the natural outworking of God's spirit as a result of a life devoted to prayer, Scripture, worship, and community.

O God Who Sends,

You have loved the world and continually communicated your message of love to us by first sending the law and the prophets, and ultimately by sending your only Son.

Now, just as the Father has sent the Son, I am sent in the power of the Holy Spirit to live out my life as a missional Christian.

Grant me the vision and courage to be faithful to this calling . . . in the name of Jesus. AMEN.

THE NEXT SEVEN DAYS

WEEK 7: Missional Service

Over the next seven days, continue to commit yourself toward the practice of making a sacred spiritual space in your daily routine in order to read the assigned Scripture, honestly reflect over your life, and pray.

DAY ONE

Begin your sacred time with a few minutes of silence. Try to clear your mind and breathe deeply.

Read John 13:14-15 and listen for God. Try going through the process of *lectio divina*. Read through the Scripture passage slowly three or four times. Write down thoughts, words, or phrases as God speaks to you.

Reflect on the ways that God has been with you recently and in your past, and give thanks to God. Enjoy these quiet moments.

Rest. Ask God to create in you a desire to know God and God's word in a deeper way.

Respond. Write down two or three concrete ways that you can serve God through acts of missional service as you are cultivating deep roots of faith.

_____
_____
_____
_____
_____
_____
_____
_____

DAY TWO

Begin your sacred time with a few minutes of silence. Try to clear your mind and breathe deeply.

Read John 13:34-35 and listen for God. Try going through the process of *lectio divina*. Read through the Scripture passage slowly three or four times. Write down thoughts, words, or phrases as God speaks to you.

_____
_____
_____
_____
_____
_____
_____
_____
_____

Reflect on the ways that God has been with you recently and in your past, and give thanks to God. Enjoy these quiet moments.

_____
_____
_____
_____
_____
_____
_____
_____
_____
_____
_____
_____

Rest. Ask God to create in you a desire to know God and God's word in a deeper way.

Respond. Write down two or three concrete ways that you can serve God through acts of missional service as you are cultivating deep roots of faith.

_____
_____
_____
_____
_____
_____
_____
_____
_____
_____

DAY THREE

Begin your sacred time with a few minutes of silence. Try to clear your mind and breathe deeply.

Read Matthew 25:34-36 and listen for God. Try going through the process of *lectio divina*. Read through the Scripture passage slowly three or four times. Write down thoughts, words, or phrases as God speaks to you.

_____
_____
_____
_____
_____
_____
_____
_____
_____

Reflect on the ways that God has been with you recently and in your past, and give thanks to God. Enjoy these quiet moments.

_____
_____
_____
_____
_____
_____
_____
_____
_____

Rest. Ask God to create in you a desire to know God and God's word in a deeper way.

Respond. Write down two or three concrete ways that you can serve God through acts of missional service as you are cultivating deep roots of faith.

DAY FOUR

Begin your sacred time with a few minutes of silence. Try to clear your mind and breathe deeply.

Read Luke 9:23 and listen for God. Try going through the process of *lectio divina*. Read through the Scripture passage slowly three or four times. Write down thoughts, words, or phrases as God speaks to you.

Reflect on the ways that God has been with you recently and in your past, and give thanks to God. Enjoy these quiet moments.

_____
_____
_____
_____
_____
_____
_____
_____
_____

Rest. Ask God to create in you a desire to know God and God's word in a deeper way.

Respond. Write down two or three concrete ways that you can serve God through acts of missional service as you are cultivating deep roots of faith.

_____
_____
_____
_____
_____
_____
_____
_____
_____
_____

DAY FIVE

Begin your sacred time with a few minutes of silence. Try to clear your mind and breathe deeply.

Read Mark 10:42-45 and listen for God. Try going through the process of *lectio divina*. Read through the Scripture passage slowly three or four times. Write down thoughts, words, or phrases as God speaks to you.

_____

_____

_____

_____

_____

_____

_____

_____

_____

Reflect on the ways that God has been with you recently and in your past, and give thanks to God. Enjoy these quiet moments.

_____

_____

_____

_____

_____

_____

_____

_____

_____

Rest. Ask God to create in you a desire to know God and God's word in a deeper way.

Respond. Write down two or three concrete ways that you can serve God through acts of missional service as you are cultivating deep roots of faith.

_____
_____
_____
_____
_____
_____
_____
_____
_____
_____

DAY SIX

Begin your sacred time with a few minutes of silence. Try to clear your mind and breathe deeply.

Read Matthew 5:13-16 and listen for God. Try going through the process of *lectio divina*. Read through the Scripture passage slowly three or four times. Write down thoughts, words, or phrases as God speaks to you.

_____
_____
_____
_____
_____
_____
_____
_____
_____

Reflect on the ways that God has been with you recently and in your past, and give thanks to God. Enjoy these quiet moments.

_____
_____
_____
_____
_____
_____
_____
_____
_____
_____

Rest. Ask God to create in you a desire to know God and God's word in a deeper way.

Respond. Write down two or three concrete ways that you can serve God through acts of missional service as you are cultivating deep roots of faith.

_____
_____
_____
_____
_____
_____
_____
_____
_____
_____
_____

DAY SEVEN

Begin your sacred time with a few minutes of silence. Try to clear your mind and breathe deeply.

Read Matthew 28:18-20 and listen for God. Try going through the process of *lectio divina*. Read through the Scripture passage slowly three or four times. Write down thoughts, words, or phrases as God speaks to you.

_____
_____
_____
_____
_____
_____
_____
_____
_____
_____

Reflect on the ways that God has been with you recently and in your past, and give thanks to God. Enjoy these quiet moments.

_____
_____
_____
_____
_____
_____
_____
_____
_____
_____

Rest. Ask God to create in you a desire to know God and God's word in a deeper way.

Respond. Write down two or three concrete ways that you can serve God through acts of missional service as you are cultivating deep roots of faith.

_____
_____
_____
_____
_____
_____
_____
_____
_____
_____
_____

Notes

[1] John Stott, *Through the Bible Through the Year*. Grand Rapids: Baker Books, 2006:311.

[2] *Christian Ethics Today*, Christmas, 2004:9.

[3] Letty M. Russell, *Church in the Round*. Louisville: Westminster John Knox Press, 1993:88

[4] Henri J. M. Nouwen, *The Inner Voice of Love*. New York: Doubleday, 1996:59-60.

[5] Robert Webber, *Journey to Jesus: The Worship, Evangelism, and Nurture Mission of the Church*. Nashville: Abingdon Press, 2001:20

[6] Kendra Creasy Dean, *Almost Christian: What the Faith of Our Teenagers Is Telling the American Church*. New York: Oxford University Press, 2010:89.

[7] Ibid: 189.

[8] Herb Miller, *Actions Speak Louder Than Verbs*. Nashville: Abingdon Press, 1989.

[9] Emil Brunner, *The Word and the World*. London: SCM Press, 1931:108.

POSTSCRIPT

Sustained by Joy and Grace

In Acts 2:42-47 we have seen the model for deep faith up close. Near the end of this passage of Scripture we read that the early Christians had "glad and generous hearts." They practiced a deeply rooted life of prayer, the study of Scripture/the apostle's teachings, worship and sharing community, and missional service to others. They practiced these things not with a sense of dread and guilt, but rather with a spirit of joy and grace. It was the joy of the Holy Spirit and the grace of the Father that enabled them to live devoted to the ways of Christ. Their example of a life of deep faith flowed naturally, and it was attractive to others!

If we attempt to live lives of devotion to Jesus apart from joy and grace, then our faith will become dull, dry, and lifeless. Without joy and grace, the sacred practices or spiritual disciplines we engage in will degenerate into a list of rules and legalistic requirements of faith. This we must resist!

It is clear from reading the gospels that joy and grace were at the heart of the life and teachings of Christ. He was born amidst the announcement of joy from the angels. He began his ministry by announcing that he had come to proclaim Good News and freedom (see Luke 4:18-19). His teachings were meant to bring abundant life to those who followed him (see John 15:11; Matthew 6:25-34).[1] So as we cultivate these sacred practices into the daily soil of our lives we must never lose our joy!

On August 27, 2011, the folks who live along the Atlantic coast experienced the awesome power of Hurricane Irene. The winds howled and the rains fell in my part of North Carolina for almost 24 hours straight. Overall, we came through the hurricane with only some downed trees and scattered power outages. After the storm passed, I went outside to survey the debris strewn all over my backyard. After a few minutes thinking I was in the clear, I noticed a very tall pine tree that had been blown over and was now leaning into a great big oak tree behind my house.

The pine tree was no more than a foot from falling across my storage building, but the top of the pine tree rested against the canopy of the big oak. Both trees leaned in the direction of my house, but the strong oak tree was preventing the tall pine from falling. The weight of the uprooted pine tree was essentially being absorbed by the mighty oak. It was at that moment I thanked God for the strong and deep root system of the oak tree. Without its deep roots, both trees would have fallen like dominoes first onto my shed and then my house! Thanks to the mighty oak tree, a disaster was averted.

Jesus concluded his epic Sermon on the Mount with these words: "Everyone then who hears these words of mine and acts on them will be like a wise man who built his house on the rock. The rains fell, the floods came, and the winds blew and beat on that house, but it did not fall, because it had been founded on rock"(Matthew 7:24-25).

It is impossible to overstate the importance of a deep root system of faith for our lives. Storms will come, and it is then that we will discover just how deep our spiritual roots have grown. We simply cannot live a sustained life of joy and hope without the deep faith and assurance of God's grace. Joy is a fruit of the Spirit (Galatians 5:22) which sustains our life through every circumstance. Joy comes *through* obedience to Christ and results *from* obedience to Christ.

Scripture calls us to live in a spirit of thanksgiving in the midst of all circumstances. Jesus tells us not to worry and to live in carefree trust of God our Father (see Philippians 4:4-8 and Matthew 6:25.)

Finally, daily dependence upon God's grace with a spirit of joy prevents us from taking ourselves too seriously! Knowing that God wants joy for our lives, knowing that God's wants to grant the desires of our hearts, and knowing that God offers us unending grace through our mistakes and sins enables us to stop sweating the small things in life.

So now this part of our *Deep Faith* journey comes to an end, but it is really a new beginning! Use the format provided here as a model to build your own daily spiritual journal for prayer, reading Scripture, and meditating on God's Word. Develop a rhythm that fits your life stage today. Take small steps and trust in God's grace.

Always remember that *as you delight yourself in the Lord,* God is pleased to give you the desires of your heart (Psalm 37:4). What better way to "delight yourself in the Lord" than to commit your way to him by cultivating deep spiritual roots through the sacred practices of prayer, Scripture, worship, community, and missional service?

Life is too precious — and too short — to be spent blown about by the daily winds of busyness, the whims of culture, or worse yet being completely uprooted because of a shallow root system.

God's Word teaches us that those who cultivate deep spiritual roots and choose to engage in a life of *Deep Faith*, will be ". . . like trees planted by streams of water, which yield their fruit in its season, and their leaves do not wither. In all they do, they prosper" (Psalm 1:3). This is a promise you can believe in and build your life upon!

Note

[1]Richard Foster, *Celebration of Discipline.* Harper & Row, San Francisco: 1988:190.

Small Group Discussion

Leader's Guide

INTRODUCTION

Scratching the Surface

One hot summer afternoon several years ago, a typical late afternoon thunderstorm rolled into the area of eastern North Carolina where I live. The rain fell with a torrential force, and the winds howled. It was very intense. Then after about 15 minutes, it was all over. When I walked outside I noticed a tree across the street had blown over in my neighbor's front yard. It wasn't a huge tree — maybe 20 feet tall — but it wasn't newly planted either.

It was a Bradford pear tree. Many people fall in love with the rich autumn color and beautiful spring blossoms of the ubiquitous Bradford pear. Bradfords grow fast, and they seem to be planted in just about every new suburban neighborhood. However, Bradford pears are also notorious for having weak wood and shallow root systems. If you're lucky, you might get 25 years out of one these Bradfords. The mighty oak tree, on the other hand, can grow over one hundred feet tall and survive several hundred years. Oak trees are known for their deep root systems and strong branches. Nature teaches us that superficial beauty combined with shallow roots simply does not stand the test of time.

I have a great suspicion that many ordinary folks today have a gnawing in their gut that life could be more. If we are honest, even among many faithful Christians there is often a nagging sense of emptiness. The rich spirituality of a living faith in Jesus Christ never developed a deep root system in their lives. As a result, what started out as tender shoots of faith have been "rooted out" by something else or blown over in stormy situations.

Such people are living life on the surface — like seeds being blown about by the winds of busyness, ambition, or popular culture. There are simply no roots deep or wide enough in place that can keep surface people connected to the true source of a thriving, fruitful life. Such people may be completely unaware that there is even a root problem — at least, until the storms of life come.

This spiritual sense of *rootlessness* begins to reveal itself with a lack of passion or interest in God and no meaningful connection with a community of faith. People become consumed with making a living, getting through school, or raising a family. Accomplishing goals and moving through the stages of life begin to fly by like mile markers along an Interstate. *And it just happens.*

Whether you call it an unintentional life or a life without proper cultivation, the result is the same: a life lived on the surface desperately in need of a spiritually-deep root system. *So how does one start over? Is there still time for deep roots to be cultivated?*

This study is for those who need a framework — a starting point — for engaging in a more intentional life and a deeper faith. For a variety of reasons we're all been there. The root issue is, *Do you want to go deeper, or not?*

Faith in Jesus should be transformative. Faith in Jesus should be alive and moving. Faith in Jesus should deeply involve the whole person — heart, soul, mind, and strength.

Church should be the community where this deep faith is encouraged, nurtured, and lived out in the context of other Christ-followers. Church should be the one safe place where we can be curious, ask questions, share doubts and struggles, and learn to breathe spiritually again. But too often it is not.

As a pastor of over twenty years, I have often been guilty of investing too much time in institutional matters while, at the same time, trying to ensure that all the diverse generations of the church live in relative peace and happiness. The fact is most pastors and lay leaders invest much time in committees and organizational structure, maintaining and improving church facilities, planning "relevant" worship services and worthy mission projects.

What is often missing in our frantic attempts to "be the church" in the challenging times of the twenty-first century is the transformation of individuals and the larger Christian community itself.

Intuitively, many of us know that we need a deeper, more relevant faith. We need a faith that plunges well beneath the surface of life. We need to allow strong, deep spiritual roots to grow each day that will sustain our life on this earth and bear fruit that lasts into eternity.

The latest car, updated smart phone, different job, or new marriage won't do. We need to discover — or rediscover — the sacred spiritual practices that cultivate a deep root system of faith for a joyful life. As these deep roots of faith grow, we will become transformed into the image of Jesus. Nothing less will do when it comes to our faith.

If you have a gnawing sense that you've been scratching the surface of life and faith — that something more is needed — then commit yourself to this *Deep Faith* study. These seven sessions will be best experienced in the context of community. We all need others along this journey toward a deeper faith. Deep faith is intensely personal but it is necessarily communal.

In order to get the most out of this study, you will need to commit yourself to the daily Scripture readings found in the Next Seven Days Journal (or card), and toward being present for each weekly session — whether it is a Sunday School class or a small group. Your presence in worship on Sunday morning is also an important part of the journey together toward a deeper faith.

Finally, as you begin — or reignite — this journey it is important to understand that the ebb and flow of life also applies to faith. As we make our way through the seasons and stages of life, deep faith in Jesus Christ will look a bit different for each one of us. Some of us are more contemplative by nature and some are more activity-centered. Teenagers, young adults, parents, and retirees all have different levels of need and availability of time. For example, an "empty nester" will likely have a different level of daily demands than a young mother of three with a full-time job.

Hence a "rule of life," i.e., an orderly way of daily experiencing God, is needed regardless of life stage in order to cultivate a deep root system. The way of grace assures us that God will meet us wherever we are and take us on an unmatched journey of faith that yields a life of fruit deeply rooted in joy and meaning.

In the first two sessions, we will become familiar with what it means to have a deeper desire for God and the necessity of building deep spiritual roots.

In the remaining sessions we will learn the early church model of cultivating deep faith that is formed by the sacred spiritual practices of prayer, Scripture, worship, community, and missional service. Finally, we will see that the way of deep faith is ultimately sustained by a spirit of joy and grace.

As you work through this study, I urge you to prayerfully ask God to create in you a growing desire for a deeper faith that is rooted in God's grace. May you come to know the breadth and depth of God the Father through Jesus Christ our Lord in the power of the Holy Spirit, who live and reigns, One God, now and forever. AMEN.

> "As you therefore have received Christ Jesus the Lord, continue to live your lives in him, rooted and built up in him and established in the faith, just as you were taught, abounding with thanksgiving." (Colossians 2:6-7)

WEEK ONE

Desire for a Deeper Faith

Read aloud the following reasons for only scratching the surface of life:
- I'm busy.
- I'm stressed.
- I'm overworked.
- I've got financial struggles.
- I honestly don't think about going deeper.
- I'm afraid of going deeper.
- I'm afraid of what I may have to give up.
- My life revolves around my family and their expectations.
- My hobbies and recreation are too important to me.
- [Other suggestions from the group.]

Ask the group: How is it that we make time for personal fitness programs, civic and community organizations, weekly social activities, children's sports activities, dance, scouts, etc., but only give a passing glance to the matter of our spiritual depth?

Ask the group to share genuine responses to the following questions:
- Are you honestly growing spiritually?
- Do you desire to have a life with more depth and meaning?
- When do you feel closest to God?

- When was that last time you wondered, "Is there something more to Christianity, to church, to knowing God than what I've been experiencing?"

Read Psalm 42:7: "Deep calls to deep at the thunder of your cataracts; all your waves and your billows have gone over me."

Ask: Is "deep calling to deep," in your life? Can you sense the very depth of who God is longing to meet the depth of who you are?

Share: Many people who consider themselves to be Christian have wandered away from the fold of God's grace and fail to return to the true Source of life on a regular basis for nourishment and guidance.

If we are finding refreshment in Christ — which is our deep well — then we will not stray far from him. On the other hand, if we discover that we have strayed away from the well then perhaps we have lost our connection with the Source of our life and we are actually searching for nourishment and fulfillment in other places.

Read the following to consider how an abundant life is necessarily related to the Source of Life.

In some farming communities, the farmers might build fences around their properties to keep livestock in and the livestock of neighboring farms out. *This is a bounded set.* But in rural communities where farms or ranches cover an enormous geographic area, fencing the property is out of the question. In (Australia) ranches are so vast that fences are superfluous. Under these conditions a farmer has to sink a bore and create a well, a precious water supply in the Outback. It is assumed that livestock, though they will stray, will never roam too far from the well, lest they die. *This is a centered set.* As long as there is a supply of clean water, the livestock will remain close by. (Michael Frost and Alan Hirsch, *The Shaping of Things to Come: Innovation and Mission for the 21st Century Church.* Peabody, Mass.: Hendrickson, 2003: 47)

Share: What keeps us coming back to our Source of life is not a list of rules or guilt, but rather love and trust. There are no rigid boundaries or fences drawn for sheep. There is the love and trust in the shepherd who will supply for all of the needs of his sheep.

Read Psalm 37:3-5. Meditate over the words slowly and deliberately.
> Trust in the LORD and do good;
> Dwell in the land and cultivate faithfulness.
> Delight yourself in the LORD;
> And He will give you the desires of your heart.
> Commit your way to the LORD,
> Trust also in Him, and He will do it. (NASB)

Read aloud the following statements. Pause after each one and ask the group to offer their own reflections and responses:
- The mechanism for "knowing God's will/desire" and experiencing the reality of God's deep presence is located in "the desires of your heart."
- This mechanism (sometimes called our intuitive nature) is activated as we "take delight in the Lord" as a regular pattern for living.
- This posture represents a relationship flowing with freedom and trust rather than a relationship that is defined by coercion, guilt, and rules.
- At the heart of a deep faith is the desire and commitment of the individual will to cultivate a life of faithfulness and delight in the Lord himself.
- Cultivating faithfulness involves building sacred practices — such as prayer and Scripture, worship and community, and missional service — into the rhythm of your life.
- Psalm 37 tells us that God is pleased to grant the desires of such a heart.

Honestly evaluate your own desires right now. Ask the group:
- Where does your delight for life come from?
- Is it ultimately from the God who created you — and all good things — or from something less?

Share: When we are delighting ourselves in God, then God is pleased to grant us the deepest desires of our hearts. Why? Because it is God who molds and shapes our desires when our hearts are open to God.

Honestly confronting our desires is the way we begin to scratch beneath the surface of life and move toward a deeper faith.

For most of us, a "rite of confession" is needed to repent from our dependence on "things and activities" that occupy our time and energy, and return to the deep well — which is Christ Jesus. If that applies to your life, then take a moment and pray the following prayer of confession.

If you use the prayer of confession for a group exercise then you will want to make a copy for each member of the group or write in on a board or power point slide.

> Heavenly Father,
> Forgive me for living my life in such a way that distracts me from knowing you.
> I confess that I have become consumed by the cares of this life rather than the things of your kingdom.
> I confess that I have lost a deep desire to know the depths of the One who created me.
> I confess that I have lost my way and need to return to the Source of my life for daily grace and sustenance.
> I confess that I need to come back to you, O God, and the caring community of your people who are the church.
> Please guide my steps and enable me to build into the rhythm of my life the sacred spiritual practices of prayer, Scripture, worship and community, and missional service with a joyful heart.
> Grant me, O God, the desire to know you better, to grow deeper roots of faith, and participate in the coming of your kingdom on earth as it is in heaven . . .
> through Jesus Christ our Lord in the power of the Holy Spirit.
> AMEN.

Before dismissing the group, review "The Next Seven Days" Journal Guide for this week (Appendix A) and encourage each member to make a commitment toward these daily Scripture readings and guided prayer

until the next small group meeting. As their leader, let them know that you will pray for each of them by name each day of the coming week.

WEEK TWO

Cultivating Deep Roots

Read Psalm 1:1-3: "Happy are those who do not follow the advice of the wicked, or take the path that sinners tread, or sit in the seat of scoffers; but their delight is in the law of the Lord, and on his law they meditate day and night. They are like trees planted by streams of water, which yield their fruit in its season, and their leaves do not wither. In all they do, they prosper."

Share: Psalm 1 paints the splendid word picture of a well-watered tree that is healthy, fruitful, and prospering. Notice the contrast between those who are wicked and those who delight in God's law, or God's ways.

Ask the group: In what ways do following the words of the wicked and the pathway of sinners and scoffers lead to a life that has a shallow root system, lacks nourishment, and ultimately withers away?

In what specific ways can you cultivate a healthy thriving environment for your life, and your family, where you enjoy a deeply rooted and fruitful life?

Share: Our lives must be intentional and properly centered toward God — who is our creator and sustainer — rather than the other "things" which we may be tempted to substitute for the well of living water.

Psalm 1 is a wake-up call for God's people to cultivate a deeper life of faith and a more intentional way of living — one that ultimately satisfies and gives meaning to the world.

Read Colossians 2:6-7: "As you therefore have received Christ Jesus the Lord, continue to live your lives in him, rooted and built up in him and established in the faith, just as you were taught, abounding with thanksgiving."

Ask the group: Did you grow up "rooted and built up" in Christian faith? If so, then describe how? What does that mean for you today? If not, how did the lack of a rooted faith affect your life then and now?

Slowly read aloud the following words that describe the kind of deeply-rooted faith mentioned in Colossians 2:6-7. Display the list, if possible.
- Received
- Continue
- Rooted
- Built
- Established
- Faith
- Taught
- Abounding

Ask the group:
- What do these action words have to contribute to your understanding of faith?
- Do you typically think of faith as a noun or a verb?
- Is faith something you "have" or something you "do"? Or both?

Share: Biblical faith involves the whole person and every aspect of the life affected by faith. Christian faith cannot be separated from other aspects of one's life. Following Christ is all-consuming. Therefore, authentic faith in Jesus means that you are deeply rooted in the ways of Christ and inextricably connected to him!

Read John 15:1-8:
> "I am the true vine, and my Father is the vinegrower. He removes every branch in me that bears no fruit. Every branch that bears fruit he prunes to make it bear more fruit. You have already been cleansed by the word that I have spoken to you. Abide in me as I abide in you. Just as the branch cannot bear fruit by itself unless it abides in the vine, neither can you unless you abide in me. I am the vine, you are the branches. Those who abide in me and I in them bear much fruit, because apart from me you can do nothing. Whoever does not abide in me is thrown away like a branch and withers; such branches are

gathered, thrown into the fire, and burned. If you abide in me, and my words abide in you, ask for whatever you wish, and it will be done for you. My Father is glorified by this, that you bear much fruit and become my disciples."

Say: The purpose of Jesus' analogy is to describe the abiding relationship between himself and his follower(s) likened to that earlier relationship between Yahweh and Israel.

Read Psalm 80:8-11:
"You brought a vine out of Egypt; you drove out the nations and planted it. You cleared the ground for it; it took deep root and filled the land. The mountains were covered with its shade, the mighty cedars with its branches; it sent out its branches to the sea, and its shoots to the River."

Say: The connection between the true vine and the branch is essential for life and intended to bear fruit. "Abide in me" means abide in my love.

The attachment of the two parties described here is not viewed as an end in itself. Rather, the purpose is to "bear fruit."

Ask the group:
- How do Christians "abide" in Christ?
- How is that "abiding" connection maintained in your own life?

Share: The bond with Christ is maintained by abiding in him and his words — historically (scripture), through the church, and through the Holy Spirit in your interior life.

Notice how the phrases "I am" and "you are" are reiterated for emphasis. There is a mutual abiding that results in much fruit. Fruit may be understood as qualities of Christian character as well as the affect of one's life upon others.

Notice that when the connection between vine and branch is broken, the result is no fruit. Nothing. The entire relationship stands under both grace (v.3) and judgment (v.6).

Ask the group: What do you do with broken-off branches that become scattered around your yard?

Say: This analogy serves to emphasize the necessity and seriousness of remaining in vital connection with Christ if fruitfulness is to continue in our lives.

Before dismissing the group, review "The Next Seven Days" Journal Guide for this week (Appendix A), and encourage each member to make a commitment toward these daily Scripture readings and guided prayer until the next small group meeting. As their leader, let them know that you will pray for each of them by name each day of the coming week.

Say a Closing Prayer:
Almighty God,
You are creator of all things, sustainer of all life, and giver of all good gifts.
Grant that we may acknowledge your presence and goodness in all times
and remain in continual connection with your son Jesus Christ,
through the power of the Holy Spirit. AMEN.

WEEK THREE

THE DEEP FAITH MODEL

Ask the group: Have you ever imagined what the ideal Christian community might look like? What are some of your ideal church's characteristics?

Leading your group in discussion, use the following headings to create a model church. Use a chalkboard or poster to record the group's responses:
- How does the model church pray?
- How does the model church approach the Bible?
- How does the model church worship?
- How does the model church love each other and share community?
- How does the model church serve its community and world?
- How does the model church extend grace toward others?
- In what ways is the model church a joyful place to be?

Read Acts 2:42-47:
> They devoted themselves to the apostles' teaching and fellowship, to the breaking of bread and the prayers. Awe came upon everyone, because many wonders and signs were being done by the apostles. All who believed were together and had all things in common; they would sell their possessions and goods and distribute the proceeds to all, as any had need. Day by day, as they spent much time together in the temple, they broke bread at home and ate their food with glad and generous hearts, praising God and having the goodwill of all the people. And day by day the Lord added to their number those who were being saved.

Say: The ancient church in the Book of Acts is the model of a missional community engaged in a deep faith in God through Jesus Christ, sustained and guided by the power of the Holy Spirit.

There are five forming principals of that early Christian community of disciples. Their deep faith was formed by the Holy Spirit through:

- *Prayer.* Our faith is formed as individuals, and in the context of community, through the practice of abiding in Christ AKA prayer. There are many ways in which we can pray. We will learn more later about forms of prayer such as centering prayer, praying the Scriptures or *lectio Divina*, breath prayers, intercessory prayer, and even praying without words (v.42).

Ask the group: What does prayer mean for you today? How can you be open to a deeper life of prayer?

- *Scripture.* Our faith is formed by the words of Holy Scripture. The early Christians were "devoted" to the apostle's teaching. The Greek word *proskartereo* means to be devoted to, to continue in, to be strong towards. These Christians were hungry for the word of God; they were strongly committed to continuing in and learning from the Scripture. Having a proper view of Scripture and being devoted to how it shapes and forms us is essential to a deep faith. This necessarily involves the regular habit of asking questions and honestly seeking to go deeper into the teachings of Scripture and their application for our lives (v.42).

Ask the group: What does the Bible mean for you today? How can you grow a desire for a deeper engagement with Scripture?

- *Worship.* Our faith is formed by gathering with fellow disciples for worship of the Triune God. Authentic worship forms deep faith within us when we gather together for the purpose of experiencing God's presence(v.46).

Ask the group: What does worship mean for you today? How can you open yourself to a deeper experience of God through the rich variety and forms of worship available to us?

- *Community.* Our faith is formed by the Holy Spirit's work of *koinonia* (Gk.) or fellowship/ community in the life of all believers. This kind of community is different than other groups in society. New Testament community involves the honest acceptance of others, the equal sharing in grace at the table as we break bread together, and working towards the common good of all (v.42).

Ask the group: What does being in community with other Christians mean for you today? How might you need to deepen you experience of Christian community?

- *Missional Service.* We are formed by our missional service to all who have need. God is a "sending" missional God, and we are God's "sent" missional people. This outward focus of service to others was a sign of the early Christians' unity and commitment to the common good of all. A deep faith in Christ involves working for justice and equality, caring for the forgotten or neglected, giving sacrificially for those in need, and sharing our spiritual gifts as we live out our lives and careers in the world (v.44-45)

Ask the group: What does living a life of service to others look like in your mind? How can you begin to deepen your understanding of God's call to live missionally as a way of life?

Discuss these final points about the model for deep faith.
- The ancient model of deep faith hinges upon the core values of prayer, Scripture, worship, community, and missional service.
- *Ultimately, the model for deep faith is sustained by a spirit of joy and grace.*
- As sinners who have been forgiven, we understand that we are formed and sustained by God's grace. Thus we gladly and generously extend God's grace to all!
- Grace was a critical aspect of the early church's favor with the people. They displayed a heart of gratitude and grace. They were

motivated and driven by love rather than rules. The deep faith pattern of daily living cannot be generated or sustained by law or guilt, but rather only by grace through the Spirit of God. v. 46-47
- The deep faith model will often, but not always, lead to a more attractive faith resulting in people being drawn in by the Holy Spirit. As faith practices grow deeper — prayer, Scripture, worship, community, missional service — the community affected becomes wider.
- The deep faith model must be grounded in God's grace and rooted in the missional love of God, who loved us and gave himself for us.
- The deep faith model cannot fully be dissected or reduced into following a prescribed system of mechanical steps.
- The model for deep faith is *a way of being* (*ethos*) that we must aspire to daily, as we stay connected and grow a more deeply-rooted faith.
- The way of deep faith will be worked out differently for each individual and each community of Christians, but it will necessarily include the core values of prayer, Scripture, worship, community, and missional service.

Before dismissing the group, review "The Next Seven Days" Journal Guide for this week (Appendix A), and encourage each member to make a commitment toward these daily Scripture readings and guided prayer until the next small group meeting. As their leader, let them know that you will pray for each of them by name each day of the coming week.

Say a Closing Prayer:
Holy God,
You have always had a people — beginning with Israel and now through your church. Although we are imperfect and weak, help us to bear with one another, forgiving one another and loving one another with Jesus Christ as our model. Together we are Christ's body and he is the living head of the Church, in the power of the Holy Spirit. AMEN.

> WEEK FOUR

FORMED BY PRAYER

Discuss: The disciples watched Jesus pray with more focus and fortitude than anyone they had ever been with. Then they watched him perform miracles and heard him teach with unrivaled power and wisdom. Soon they concluded that what Jesus said and did was connected to how he prayed.

Next to Jesus, it was painfully obvious that the disciples knew nothing about prayer. So one day they made a request to Jesus, "Lord, teach us to pray" (Luke 11:1). What Jesus taught them is what we often today call "the Lord's Prayer."

"Our Father which art in heaven, Hallowed be thy name. Thy kingdom come, Thy will be done in earth, as it is in heaven. Give us this day our daily bread. And forgive us our debts, as we forgive our debtors. And lead us not into temptation, but deliver us from evil. For thine is the kingdom, and the power, and the glory, for ever. Amen." (Matthew 6:9-13 KJV)

If we're honest, we also know nothing about prayer. Prayer is a mystery and Jesus did not try to explain it away. What Jesus did was model a life of communion with God, and in so doing clearly demonstrate the necessity of prayer in the life of his followers.

Ask the group:
- How do you define prayer?
- What does it mean for you to pray?
- What forms of prayer do you practice?
- What do you need to learn about prayer?

Read Mark 1:35: "In the morning, while it was still very dark, he (Jesus) got up and went out to a deserted place, and there he prayed."

Say: Jesus modeled for us a life of prayer. Jesus often prayed before healed and gave thanks before he broke bread.

Ask the group: Do you currently have a pattern or routine for daily prayer? If so, describe?

Say: The beginning and ending of all prayer is "the act of submitting my will to God's will." In between, there are many different kinds of prayers and many different ways in which to pray. At the most basic level, to pray is to change. As we open ourselves to the will and purposes of God, communion with God changes us. We are always learning more about how to pray.

Discuss: The following are some different ways that we can encounter God through prayer:

Listening Prayer — Being still and silent before God is perhaps counterintuitive for many of us. Just try it. Ask nothing. Say nothing. Just listen. (See Psalm; 25:4-5; 27:14; 31:24; 37:7; 46:10-11.)

Wordless Prayer — Perhaps our purest prayers occur when we have no idea what to pray. It is then that the Holy Spirit takes over and utters prayers that are too deep for words (see Romans 8:26-27).

Spontaneous Prayer — Whenever someone or some circumstance comes into your mind, simply offer that person or circumstance, over to God. Pray what is on your heart. Anytime. Anywhere. This is one aspect of how we "pray without ceasing" (see 1 Thessalonians 5:17) throughout the ordinariness of daily life.

Confessional Prayer — We are all sinners in need of God's forgiveness and grace. We need to ask God to cleanse us from known and unknown sin. The ancient church fathers and mothers would pray over and over throughout the day a prayer that has come to be known simply as the Jesus Prayer: "Lord Jesus Christ, Son of God, have mercy on me a sinner." (See also Psalm 51:10)

Intercessory Prayer — This is the kind of prayer where we lift up others and their particular needs or circumstances before God (see Philippians 4:6-7 and 1 Corinthians 3:9). You may choose to make a list of those persons and concern that you want to offer to God in prayer.

Corporate Prayer — Besides our individual private prayer, we need to pray in the company of other disciples of Jesus. There is a divine power available "when two or three are gathered in my name," Jesus said in Matthew 18:19-20. The early Christians regularly devoted themselves to praying together (see Acts 1:14; 2:42; 4:31; 6:2-6; 16:16; 20:36). This is where the church connects with the power of God's Holy Spirit, and it cannot be underestimated!

Persistent Prayer — Don't stop praying! Don't give up. Jesus said, "Ask, seek, knock . . . " We are to "pray without ceasing, give thanks in all circumstances; for this is the will of God in Christ Jesus for you" (1 Thessalonians 5:17-18).

Scripture Prayer — *Lectio divina* is a Latin phrase meaning divine or sacred reading. *Lectio divina* provides us with a way to intertwine prayer with the Scriptures. It is a way of praying that dates back to many of the early followers of Jesus. There are many beautiful prayers already contained within the pages of Scripture. Furthermore, reading Scripture slowly and contemplatively enables us to offer the Word of God back to God. Then we allow God to speak to us through the words of Scripture. A simplified version of *lectio divina* is as follows:

1) Read. (*lectio*) Select a short passage of Scripture and before reading take a few moments of silence. Now read slowly through the passage once allowing it to simply well up within you. Spend another moment in silence.

2) Reflect. (*meditatio*) Read the passage a second time and reflect upon how these words touch your life today. *What do I need to hear in this passage? Is there a word or phrase that jumps out at me?*

3) Respond. (*oratorio*) Read the passage for a third time and listen for how the word or phrases may be speaking to where you are in your life right now. Listen for what God is calling for in your life through the Scripture. Now you are ready to pour out your heart in response to God's word. Let the Scripture draw out your honest emotion. Write down how God wants you to respond to what you have heard.

4) Rest. (*contemplatio*) Now simply rest in God's word and in God's acceptance and grace. Submit your will to God's will and delight yourself in the Lord.

5) Resolve. (*incarnatio*) As a result of your encounter with God through praying the Scripture, resolve now to act upon the word that God has given you. Throughout the day remind yourself of this experience of God's presence, and continue your resolve to go deeper in faithful obedience to God's word. (Adapted from Barton, Ruth Haley. *Sacred Rhythms: Arranging Our Lives for Spiritual Transformation.* Downers Grove, IL: InterVarsity Press, 2006: 54-61.)

Say: The most important lesson about prayer is not about *how* we pray, but *that* we pray! *Keep your focus on the person, not the process!* Prayer is more than communication with God — talking and listening. Prayer is a mysterious and deep *communion* with God that cannot be reduced to a formula.

We should feel the grace and freedom to try different approaches to prayer. Adapt a daily and weekly routine or "rule of life" that fits the life stage you happen to be at right now.

Ask the group: How might being at different stages(teen, twenties, mid-life, retired) in life affect the way that you pray?

Now, read the following verses that precede the "Lord's Prayer" in Matthew 6:5-8:

> And whenever you pray, do not be like the hypocrites; for they love to stand and pray in the synagogues and at the street corners, so that they may be seen by others. Truly I tell you, they have received their reward. But whenever you pray, go into your room and shut the door and pray to your Father who is in secret; and your Father who sees in secret will reward you. When you are praying, do not heap up empty phrases as the Gentiles do; for they think that they will be heard because of their many words. Do not be like them, for your Father knows what you need before you ask him.

Ask the group: So, if your Father already knows what you need before you ask him, why pray?

- We pray in order to commune with the God who loves us and created us!
- We pray to enjoy the fellowship and peace that passes all understanding!
- We pray to bring before our Heavenly Father the needs of our lives and the needs of others.
- We pray in order to submit our will to God's will!
- Prayer changes us!
- So be creative, intentional, and above all, just pray!

Before dismissing the group, review "The Next Seven Days" Journal Guide for this week (Appendix A), and encourage each member to make a commitment toward these daily Scripture readings and guided prayer until the next small group meeting. As their leader, let them know that you will pray for each of them by name each day of the coming week.

Say a Closing Prayer:
Heavenly Father,
To know you is to pray, to love you is to pray, to serve you is to pray, to follow you is to pray.
Grant that we may learn to pray without ceasing so that our lives might become a prayer lived unto you each day, in the name of Jesus Christ our Lord, who lives and reigns with you and the Holy Spirit, one God, forever and ever. AMEN.

WEEK FIVE

Formed by Scripture

Share: The first thing Luke, the author of Acts, tells us in chapter two is: "They devoted themselves to the apostle's teaching . . ."

The Holy Spirit began teaching the people through the apostles whom Jesus had anointed and trained. There were over 3,000 new converts at Pentecost who needed instruction on how to live as Christ-followers!

So God opened a huge class for the instruction of these new believers, and the apostles were the teachers. These new Christ-followers were starting from scratch in the ways of Jesus, so they needed to start with the basics.

In the Book of Acts, Luke uses the Greek word *mathetai* some twenty-two times in describing the church. The word means disciples, learners, or pupils.

Ask the group: Think back to your saving experience with Jesus. Did you receive teaching in the Way of Jesus following your conversion?

If so, how was that teaching formative for your faith? If not, how have you learned the ways of Christ since then?

Do you now consider yourself to be a "disciple/learner" of Jesus?

Discuss: There was a lot to learn for these new followers of Jesus. Much was at stake for the success of this new movement with Jesus now gone from their midst. But even though these new converts had been mystically and powerfully moved by God at Pentecost, they did not get a free pass to stop using their minds. Their *emotional* experience with God's Spirit did not negate their intellect.

On the contrary, they were compelled to embrace *learning* and receiving instruction from the Apostles. So from the earliest days of the church, it is clear that God wants Christians to use their minds and exercise their intellect as disciples of Jesus. In fact, this is part of fulfilling the Great Commandment — to love God with your heart, soul, *mind*, and strength.

This learning dimension of cultivating a deep faith and being formed by Scripture is just as important today is it was in the first century.

Ask the group: At what stage of biblical learning would you consider yourself to be in terms of understanding Jesus and following his ways? (Beginner, Novice, Seeker, Serious Disciple, Stumbling Along)

Discuss: Biblical illiteracy abounds these days. We can no longer assume that people know what we're talking about when we mention Jesus and the Bible. The chances are high that your children and grandchildren will know less about the Bible and ways of Jesus than you do — unless we commit our lives toward being formed by Scripture.

Gary Burge, Professor of New Testament at Wheaton College, says in his book The Greatest Story Never Read: "spiritual life has become less a matter of learning than it is a matter of experiencing. This has resulted in Christian ministries that put less premium on education than they do on personal development and therapeutic wholeness."

He goes on to conclude that, "Christian faith is not being built on the firm foundation of hard-won thoughts, ideas, history, or theology. Spirituality is being built on private emotional attachments."

Ask the group: Do you agree with the above statements? Why or why not?

Share: The modern approach to spirituality is in direct contrast to the way that Luke described the faith of the early followers of Jesus. They devoted themselves to the apostles' teaching — not simply as isolated individuals, but also in community with one another.

In Acts 17:11-12, Paul commended the Bereans for having a more "noble character" than the Thessalonians because they "received the message with great eagerness and examined the Scriptures every day to see if what Paul said was true."

Ask the group: Do you find the Bible boring, incomprehensible, or exciting? Why? How eager are you to examine the Scriptures?

Say: The invitation Jesus gave to people was "follow Me." This implies motion and movement. Again, the very word "disciple" means pupil or learner.

This word is used some 248 times in the four gospels and 22 times in the Book of Acts! This is what Jesus had in mind for us — an active, living, growing relationship — not a passive, self-serving existence.

Perhaps you've heard the old cliché that churches are "a mile wide and an inch deep." The only way out of this shallow mediocrity is to become committed to the process of spiritual formation — which is a critical aspect of deep faith.

Ask the group: Are you willing to cultivate the personal discipline of reading the Bible on a weekly — and perhaps daily — basis? Would you be willing to join a regular Bible study group in our church? If you cannot find one, then perhaps you can begin one yourself!

Discuss: The Bible is more accessible to us than at any other time in history. What we need is a hunger for learning and applying its truth.

Perhaps we need to admit that the primary reason we don't make time to learn God's word is that it's not very important to us.

Being formed by Scripture doesn't take a degree in theology — it just requires a little desire and commitment toward learning. It can happen at home in front of an open Bible, reading a chapter a day. It can happen in a Sunday School class or a small group of other willing disciples of Jesus.

Share with the group these answers to the question: How can I begin studying the Bible?
- Read through one of the four gospels using a highlighter to underline words and verses that speak to you.
- Take a small book of the Bible such as James or Philippians and read it through keeping a journal for taking notes.
- Use a Bible commentary to do a verse-by-verse study of a section of Scripture.
- Spend an entire month reading through the Sermon on the Mount (Matthew 5-7).
- Read through the entire Bible in one year.
- Read a Proverb or Psalm each day.
- Memorize a verse of Scripture each week or month.

Before dismissing the group, review "The Next Seven Days" Journal Guide for this week (Appendix A), and encourage each member to make a commitment toward these daily Scripture readings and guided prayer until the next small group meeting. As their leader, let them know that you will pray for each of them by name each day of the coming week.

Say a Closing Prayer:
> Gracious God,
> Your words are a light unto our path; like a compass, they guide us and point us in the way we should go. Help us desire your Word more and more, and to take our delight in its teachings for our lives. Thank you for your wonderful words of life, through Jesus Christ the Living Word, by the breath of the Holy Spirit. AMEN.

WEEK SIX

FORMED BY WORSHIP AND COMMUNITY

Say: The worship of God takes many forms and styles in the Bible, just as it does across the world today. Sometimes the congregation is small, and the preacher is a layperson; sometimes the congregation numbers in the thousands, and the music is accompanied by an orchestra; sometimes the worshipers are in jeans and shorts as they sing to the driving beat of electric guitars and drums; sometimes the congregation is silent and contemplative.

Yet no matter the size, style, or culture of a congregation, worship is meant to be at the center of our life together as the church and as individual Christians. It was certainly at the center of the life of the early Christians.

Read Acts 2:46: " . . . they spent much time in the temple, they broke bread together in homes (a reference to the practice of the Lord's Supper) and they also ate food with generous hearts, praising God . . . ."

Say: For the earliest Christians, worship and spending time in community with one another was not just an opportunity that came once a week on Sunday mornings! It was a necessity for their spiritual survival!

Ask the group: Do you feel a fresh desire to come together with other believers for worship? Why or why not? In your own words, what is worship? Do you sense God's presence more often when you are alone or when you are gathered with other Christians?

Discuss: Richard Foster describes worship as "the human response to the divine initiative . . ." It is God who seeks, draws, and persuades his children to come to him. (See the Genesis account, the Parable of the Prodigal Son, crucifixion — John 12:32.) "Worship is kindled within us only when the Spirit of God touches our human spirit" — Spirit touching spirit (The Celebration of Discipline. Harper & Rowe, San Francisco 1988:158).

In worship, we recognize that God has a claim, and we have a need. God's claim on us comes from two fundamental realities: *God created us, and God redeemed us.* When we recognize both God's claim on our lives and our sense of need, we are able to open up ourselves to the will of God for our life.

Read Romans 12:1-2:
"I appeal to you therefore, brothers and sisters, by the mercies of God, to present your bodies as a living sacrifice, holy and acceptable to God, which is your spiritual worship. Do not be conformed to this world, but be transformed by the renewing of your minds, so that you may discern what is the will of God — what is good and acceptable and perfect."

Discuss: The writer of Hebrews calls us "to offer to God an acceptable worship with reverence and awe; for indeed our God is a consuming fire" (12:28-29).

In recognizing who God is, we are to approach God with the wonder of a child. Think about those times when people in the Scripture experienced the awesome reality of God:
- Moses had to take his shoes off because he was on holy ground.
- Job was brought to say, "My ears had heard of you, but now my eyes have seen you."
- Isaiah said, "I am ruined: My eyes have seen the King, the Lord Almighty."
- When Thomas saw the resurrected Jesus, he proclaimed, "My Lord and my God."
- And when John sees the Christ in the first chapter of Revelation he says, "I fell at his feet as though dead."

Ask the group: When have you recognized God's holiness and claim on your life?

Say: Jesus called people to a radical and public response to his preaching of the Good News. Simply put, worship should change us.

Ask the group: How have you responded to God through a recent worship experience?

Say: In the Book of Acts, worship for the early Christians was both formal and informal. They worshiped in the temple and in their homes. It was also both joyful and reverent.

Ask the group: Do you enjoy and appreciate different forms and expressions of worship? Why or Why not?

Say: The early Christian community emphasized corporate worship — gathering together as a group and gathering with a unity of spirit that transcended their individualism (Acts 2:42-47, Hebrews 10:25, Philippians 3:15). Isaac Pennington said that when God's people gather for worship they are like "a heap of fresh and burning coals warming one another as a great strength and freshness and vigor of life flows through into all."

Ask the group: Do you find this to be true? Why or why not?

Discuss: At our best moments — when we get past ourselves to share the deep life in Christ with others — we're given a little taste of heaven on earth in this experience of sharing. It is the Greek word *koinonia*. *Koinonia* has to do with the basic idea of fellowship and sharing community.

James Packer describes it this way:
"Christian fellowship is two-dimensional, and it has to be vertical before it can be horizontal. We must know the reality of fellowship with the Father and with his Son Jesus Christ before we can know the reality of fellowship with each other in our common relationship to God (1 John 1:3). The person who is not in fellowship with the Father and the Son is no Christian at all, and so cannot share with Christians the realities of their fellowship." (James Packer, *Your Father Loves You*, Harold Shaw Publishers, 1986.)

Above all else, our *koinonia* is unique not because it is something we create, but because it something given to us by God himself. So we must always remember that God's gift of fellowship with him and with one another always trumps any other concern or issue we may want to elevate above the gift of *koinonia*.

Koinonia is the bond which binds Christians to each other, to Christ, to the Spirit, and to God the Father. Nothing happens to us alone because we are all bound together by this *koinonia* in the church.

Read John 13:34-35: "I give you a new commandment, that you love one another. Just as I have loved you, you also should love one another. By this everyone will know that you are my disciples . . ."

Ask the group: How should genuine worship of God affect both the life of the individual Christian and the collective body of the Church?

Before dismissing the group, review "The Next Seven Days" Journal Guide for this week (Appendix A), and encourage each member to make a commitment toward these daily Scripture readings and guided prayer until the next small group meeting. As their leader, let them know that you will pray for each of them by name each day of the coming week.

Say a Closing Prayer:
Holy God,
You alone are worthy to be praised; you alone are worthy to be worshiped. Help us approach you — individually and collectively — with a sincere spirit, honestly seeking after truth, and open to being transformed by the living Lord Jesus Christ through the power of the Holy Spirit. AMEN.

WEEK SEVEN

Formed by Missional Service

Say: So far, the sacred practices in the life of the early church — prayer, Scripture, worship and community — refer to life on the inside, to the church's interior life together. They tell us virtually nothing about the church's outreach to the world if we look only at Acts 2:42.

The early Christians were also committed to mission, but it's not until Acts 2:47 that we pick up on this fact.

Read Acts 2:47: "(they were) . . . praising God and having the goodwill of all the people. And day by day the Lord added to their number those who were being saved."

Discuss: Acts 2:47 teaches us three important lessons about the early church's outreach:

- First, it was the Lord himself who did it. "The Lord added to their number" says verse 42. Of course, he did it through the preaching of the apostles, the daily witness of church members, and their common life of love with one another. But it was GOD who added to their number. Only GOD can add people to the church.

- Second, the Lord added to their number . . . "those who were being saved." Notice he didn't add to their number without saving them, nor did he save them without adding them to the church. In other words, salvation and church membership, i.e., deep connection to the community of believers, still go together.

- Third, the Lord added to their number those who were being saved . . . "day by day." The early Christians did not regard evangelism and mission to be separate and occasional activities of the church. Every single day people were being added to the church.

(John Stott, *Through the Bible Through the Year*. Grand Rapids: Baker Books, 2006:311)

Ask the group: Do you think we need to rediscover this phenomenon today in our church?

Discuss: The mission frontier has moved from the foreign field to local communities. The missional church of today now meets the world through the lives of its own members! *This is absolutely crucial to understand if we are to re-orient ourselves — and our church — for participating in God's mission to the world today.*

The cultural landscape has changed. Today is a new era. Everything we do as individual Christians and as a church should be shaped by our basic understanding of missional service. We must begin to see our identity as a congregation being shaped primarily from a biblical sense of mission rather than from old denominational systems or a North American cultural sense of identity.

Deep faith requires us to view ourselves as "missional Christians." We must move from an understanding of our faith as disciples who occasionally do mission projects to a people who view our lives as being on mission right where we live 24/7!

Ask the group: What is your current view of outreach and mission as a part of your faith? How has your view of missonal service changed over the years?

Discuss: Beginning with Abraham, God intended to establish God's reign in all the earth through a people. Israel was to be that people — a missionary people, a light unto all other nations. Even when Israel as a whole refused God's mission, God did not abandon the idea that the reign — or the kingdom — of God must have a people. God's kingdom is revealed in and through the lives of God's people. That's how God has chosen it to be.

God's mission continued through the sending of his son Jesus Christ, and the community of disciples Jesus established AKA "the church." It is more biblical to say the Church doesn't *have* a mission, but rather the church *participates in God's always unfolding mission!*

So, what is the mission of the church?

It is to embody the gospel of Christ in the world, to proclaim it to the world, to enact it for the world, and to anticipate God's future kingdom when all will be under the reign of Christ. (Robert Webber, *Journey to Jesus.* Abingdon Press, Nashville, 2001:20)

Ask the group: Where are you called to share the Gospel of Christ? How are you currently engaged in God's mission?

Read Acts 1:8: "You will be my witnesses in Jerusalem, and in all Judea and Samaria, and to the ends of the earth."

Say: Jesus was saying, begin at home. Start with the people closest to you right here in your own community. Then he says, go to your county and state. And ultimately, I want you to go beyond all borders to the ends of the earth!

Share with those in your immediate circle. That's the starting point. Your mission starts at home, in your own neighborhood, in your own community. God wants you to go to your friends, your family, your coworkers, your neighbors, and anybody who randomly crosses your path.

Ask the group: What are some ways that you can say to others, "This is what God did for me in my life."

Say: Dare to reach beyond your comfort zone. Christians of deep faith are called to build bridges, not walls. God's love demands that we move beyond our comfort zone to people with different backgrounds and educational levels, different languages and economics levels. We must be willing to take risks in order to get the message out.

Ask the group: What are some ways that I might need to dare to reach beyond my comfort zone? Who are the people that fit into this category in my life?

Say: Care about the whole world. We must care because God cares about the whole world. "For God so loved the world that he gave his one Son . . ." (John 3:16).

Read Matthew 28:19: "Go therefore, and make disciples of all nations, baptizing them in the name of the Father and of the Son and of the Holy Spirit, and teaching them to obey everything that I have commanded you."

Discuss: Jesus intended this command to be for all his followers. If you're a Christian, then you are sent on mission to live in this world just as Jesus was sent on mission by his Father. You cannot care about your immediate world without caring about the whole world, because the world is here among us!

Emil Brunner said, "As a fire exists by burning, the church exists by mission." God's mission today is taking place in and through the lives of those who are the Church — as the Father has sent the Son, the Son has sent the people of God in the power of the Holy Spirit that the world might believe!

As a group, make a list of the ways that God might be calling you and your church to live lives of deepfaith through missional service. (Use a chalkboard or poster to record your responses.)

Before dismissing the group, review "The Next Seven Days" Journal Guide for this week (Appendix A), and encourage each member to make a lifelong commitment toward daily Scripture reading and prayer.

Say: The *Deep Faith* journey has only begun. It is a lifetime calling to cultivate the deep spiritual rhythms of prayer and Scripture, worship and community, missional service sustained by joy. Stay connected to your roots. "Delight yourself in the Lord, and he will give you the desires of your heart."

Say a Closing Prayer:
O God who Sends,
You have loved the world and continually communicated your message of love to us by first sending the law and the prophets and ultimately by sending your only Son. Now, just as the Father has sent the Son, we are sent in the power of the Holy Spirit to live out our lives as missional Christians. Grant us the vision and courage to be faithful to this calling . . . In the name of Jesus we pray. AMEN.

WEEK SEVEN POSTSCRIPT

Sustained by Joy and Grace

In Acts 2:42-47 we have seen the model for deep faith up close. Near the end of this passage of Scripture we read that the early Christians had "glad and generous hearts." They practiced a deeply rooted life of prayer, the study of Scripture/the apostle's teachings, worship and sharing community, and missional service to others. They practiced these things not with a sense of dread and guilt, but rather with a spirit of joy and grace.

It was the joy of the Holy Spirit and the grace of the Father that enabled them to live devoted to the ways of Christ. If we attempt to live lives of devotion to Jesus apart from joy and grace, then our faith will become dull, dry, and lifeless. Without joy and grace, the sacred practices or spiritual disciplines we engage in will degenerate into a list of rules and legalistic requirements of faith.

It is clear from reading the gospels that joy and grace were at the heart of the life and teachings of Christ. He was born amidst the announcement of joy from the angels. He began his ministry by announcing that he had come to proclaim Good News and freedom (see Luke 4:18-19). His teachings were meant to bring abundant life to those who followed him (see John 15:11; Matthew 6:25-34).

Therefore, we simply cannot live a sustained life of deep faith without the hope of joy and the confident assurance of God's grace. Joy is a fruit of the Spirit (Galatians 5:22) which sustains our life through every circumstance.

Joy comes through *obedience to Christ and results* from *obedience to Christ.* Scripture calls us to live in a spirit of thanksgiving in the midst of all circumstances. Jesus tells us not to worry and to live in carefree trust of God (Philippians 4:4-8; Matthew 6:25)!

And finally, dependence upon God's grace with a spirit of joy prevents us from taking ourselves too seriously! Knowing that God wants joy for our lives and offers us unending grace through our mistakes and sins enables us to stop sweating the small things in life.

Ask the group: In what ways might you begin to practice more joy and gladness in your daily life at home, at work, at play, and at church?

Say: Always remember that as you delight yourself in the Lord, God is pleased to give you the desires of your heart (Psalm 37:4). What better way to "delight yourself in the Lord" than to commit your way to him by cultivating deep roots through the sacred spiritual practices of prayer, Scripture, worship, community, and missional service?

Life is too precious — and too short — to be spent blown about by the winds of busyness, the whims of our culture, or worse yet being blown over because of a shallow root system. God's Word teaches us that those who cultivate deep roots through sacred spiritual practices and choose to engage in a life of deep faith will be "like trees planted by streams of water, which yield their fruit in its season, and their leaves do not wither. In all they do, they prosper" (Psalm 1:3).

APPENDIX A

"The Next Seven Days" Journal Guides

THE NEXT SEVEN DAYS

WEEK 1

Over the next seven days, commit yourself toward making a sacred spiritual space in your daily routine in order to read the assigned Scripture, honestly reflect over your life, and pray.

• This is only the beginning of the journey! Just read and pray over the assigned Scripture, and begin listening for God. Read the Scripture passage slowly two or three times. Don't try to do any more than this during the first week. Write down thoughts or notes as God speaks.

• Reflect on the ways that God has been with you recently and in your past, and give thanks to God. Rest in this daily practice — whether it lasts two minutes or ten minutes. This is the beginning of cultivating a new sacred rhythm into your daily life.

• Close your time by asking God to create in you a deeper desire to know God — as Father, Son, and Holy Spirit — thereby cultivating a life of deeper faith.

DAY ONE:	Proverbs 19:2
DAY TWO:	Psalm 10:3-4, 17-18
DAY THREE:	Psalm 73:24-26
DAY FOUR:	Psalm 42:1-2, 7
DAY FIVE:	Psalm 143:6, 8-10
DAY SIX:	1 Timothy 2:3-4
DAY SEVEN:	Psalm 37:3-5

THE NEXT SEVEN DAYS

WEEK 2

Over the next seven days, commit yourself toward making a sacred spiritual space in your daily routine in order to read the assigned Scripture, honestly reflect over your life, and pray.

• Begin your sacred time with a few minutes of silence. Try to clear your mind and breathe deeply.

• Read and pray over the assigned Scripture and begin listening for God. Read the Scripture passage slowly two or three times. Write down thoughts or notes as God speaks to you. What words seem to jump off the page at you?

• Reflect on the ways that God has been with you recently and in your past, and give thanks to God. Rest in this daily practice — whether it lasts two minutes or ten minutes. Enjoy these quiet moments. You are cultivating a new sacred rhythm into your daily life.

• Close your time by asking God to create in you a deeper desire to know God and cultivate a deeply rooted faith.

DAY ONE:	Psalm 1:1-3
DAY TWO:	Jeremiah 17:7-8
DAY THREE:	Isaiah 11:1-10
DAY FOUR:	Colossians 2:6-7
DAY FIVE:	Matthew 13:3-9
DAY SIX:	John 15:4-5
DAY SEVEN:	Ephesians 3:16-17

THE NEXT SEVEN DAYS

WEEK 3

Over the next seven days, commit yourself toward the practice of making a sacred spiritual space in your daily routine in order to read the assigned Scripture, honestly reflect over your life, and pray.

• Begin your sacred time with a few minutes of silence. Try to clear your mind and breathe deeply.

• Read and pray over the assigned Scripture, and begin listening for God. Read the Scripture passage slowly two or three times.

• Write down thoughts or notes as God speaks to you. What words seem to jump off the page at you?

• Reflect on the ways that God has been with you recently and in your past, and give thanks to God. Rest in this daily practice. Try to build your time up to 15 minutes. Enjoy these quiet moments. You are cultivating deeper roots into the rhythm of your daily life.

• Close your time by asking God to create in you a desire to know God in a deeper relationship.

DAY ONE:	Acts 2:42-27
DAY TWO:	Acts 4:31
DAY THREE:	Acts 4:32-35
DAY FOUR:	Acts 8:35-38
DAY FIVE:	Acts 10:34-36
DAY SIX:	Acts 15:30-35
DAY SEVEN:	Acts 20:32-38

THE NEXT SEVEN DAYS

WEEK 4

Over the next seven days, continue to commit yourself toward the practice of making a sacred spiritual space in your daily routine in order to read the assigned Scripture, honestly reflect over your life, and pray.

- Begin your sacred time with a few minutes of silence. Try to clear your mind, and breathe deeply.

- Read and pray over the assigned Scripture, and begin listening for God. Using the process of *lectio divina*, read through the Scripture passage slowly three or four times. Write down thoughts, words, or phrases as God speaks to you.

- Enjoy these quiet moments. Reflect on the ways that God has been with you recently, and in your past, and give thanks to God. Rest and respond at the end of praying the Scripture. You are cultivating deeper roots into the rhythm of your daily life.

- Close your time by asking God to create in you a desire to know God in a deeper relationship.

DAY ONE:	Jeremiah 29:11-14a
DAY TWO:	Matthew 7:7-11
DAY THREE:	Psalm 46:10-11
DAY FOUR:	1 Thessalonians 5:17-18
DAY FIVE:	Philippians 4:6-7
DAY SIX:	Matthew 6:5-8
DAY SEVEN:	Matthew 6:9-13

THE NEXT SEVEN DAYS

WEEK 5

Over the next seven days, continue to commit yourself toward the practice of making a sacred spiritual space in your daily routine in order to read the assigned Scripture, honestly reflect over your life, and pray.

- Begin your sacred time with a few minutes of silence. Try to clear your mind, and breathe deeply.

- Read and pray over the assigned Scripture, and begin listening for God. Try going through the process of *lectio divina*. Read through the Scripture passage slowly three or four times. Write down thoughts, words, or phrases as God speaks to you. What seems to jump off the page at you?

- Enjoy these quiet moments. Reflect on the ways that God has been with you recently and in your past, and give thanks to God. Rest and respond at the end of praying the Scripture. You are cultivating deeper roots into the rhythm of your daily life.

- Close your time by asking God to create in you a desire to know God and God's word in a deeper way.

DAY ONE:	Matthew 7:24-29
DAY TWO:	Acts 17:10-13
DAY THREE:	Hebrews 4:12
DAY FOUR:	2 Timothy 3:16-17
DAY FIVE:	Colossians 2:6-7
DAY SIX:	Psalm 1:1-3
DAY SEVEN:	Psalm 119:9, 11, 105

THE NEXT SEVEN DAYS

WEEK 6

Over the next seven days, continue to commit yourself toward the practice of making a sacred spiritual space in your daily routine in order to read the assigned Scripture, honestly reflect over your life, and pray.

- Begin your sacred time with a few minutes of silence. Try to clear your mind, and breathe deeply.

- Read and pray over the assigned Scripture and begin listening for God. Using the process of *lectio divina*, read through the Scripture passage slowly three or four times. Write down thoughts, words, or phrases as God speaks to you. What seems to jump off the page at you?

- Reflect on the ways that God has been with you, and give thanks. Rest and respond at the end of praying the Scripture. Consider concrete ways that you can worship God more faithfully and build a deeper sense of community with other Christians. You are cultivating deeper roots into your daily life.

- Close your time by asking God to create in you a desire to know God and God's word in a deeper way.

DAY ONE:	John 4:23-24
DAY TWO:	Romans 12:1-2
DAY THREE:	Hebrews 10:24-25
DAY FOUR:	Hebrews 12:28-29
DAY FIVE:	Matthew 14:22-33
DAY SIX:	2 Corinthians 13:11-13
DAY SEVEN:	Galatians 3:26-28

THE NEXT SEVEN DAYS

WEEK 7

Over the next seven days, continue to commit yourself toward the practice of making a sacred spiritual space in your daily routine in order to read the assigned Scripture, honestly reflect over your life, and pray.

- Begin your sacred time with a few minutes of silence. Try to clear your mind, and breathe deeply.

- Read and pray over the assigned Scripture, and begin listening for God. Try going through the process of *lectio divina*. Read through the Scripture passage slowly three or four times. Write down thoughts, words, or phrases as God speaks to you. What seems to jump off the page at you?

- Enjoy these quiet moments. Reflect on the ways that God has been with you recently and in your past, and give thanks to God. Rest and respond at the end of praying the Scripture. Consider concrete ways that you can serve God through acts of missional service as you are cultivating deep roots of faith.

- Close your time by asking God to create in you a desire to know and serve God and in a way that cultivates lasting deep roots of faith.

DAY ONE:	John 13:12-15
DAY TWO:	John 13:34-35
DAY THREE:	Luke 10:25-37
DAY FOUR:	Luke 9:23-24
DAY FIVE:	Mark 10:42-45
DAY SIX:	Matthew 5:13-16
DAY SEVEN:	Acts 4:32-35

APPENDIX B

"Order of Meeting" for a Small Group Experience

I. Welcome . . . with opening words of hospitality and fellowship. Make sure that all member of the group have been introduced.

II. Clarify . . . the purpose of the group. This is crucial. Many well-meaning Bible study groups spend much of their time "chasing rabbits" and gossiping about other people. Yes, it's true!

As the leader, make sure that your group will meet together for the next seven weeks to seek a deeper desire for God and to cultivate spiritual practices that grow deeper roots of faith in our lives. It's up to you to keep the group focused!

During the first meeting, establish a basic covenant and then review the covenant in future meetings. Remember that as the leader you must model and reinforce these principles. And always stress that the primary goal for your group is spiritual formation, not passing along information!

DEEP FAITH

Group Covenant

- By God's grace, I will be present and on time for each meeting over the next seven weeks.

- By God's grace, I will support and pray for the other members of this group and maintain a safe and confidential environment for questions and sharing.

- By God's grace, I will intentionally set aside a regular time for prayer and meditation over the daily Scripture readings.

- By God's grace, I will welcome the Holy Spirit and seek to practice the presence of God in my daily life.

- By God's grace, I will seek to exercise my spiritual gifts and serve others wherever I am.

- By God's grace, I will seek to love God with all that I am and love my neighbor as myself.

- By God's grace, I will joyfully live each day to the fullest and seek to be the presence of Christ in my family and community.

III. Pray . . . before you begin each session. Begin with a centering prayer asking God to open each person's mind and heart as God speaks.

IV. Follow . . . the leader's guide for each session. Read and add your own notes as you work through the outline. Always read the Scripture passages and ask the questions that follow. Encourage any and all responses and questions, but try to keep the group moving along with the lesson. Be sensitive to the time. Honor the agreed upon start and ending time.

V. Conclude . . . by asking for prayer requests and any specific areas that need to be concentrated upon during the coming week. Remind each member to follow along with the next seven days of Scripture readings, and to pray for each other. Close by asking someone to lead a prayer followed by the group sharing in the Lord's Prayer together.

Our Father which art in heaven, Hallowed be thy name.
Thy kingdom come, Thy will be done in earth, as it is in heaven.
Give us this day our daily bread. And forgive us our debts,
 as we forgive our debtors.
And lead us not into temptation, but deliver us from evil.
For thine is the kingdom, and the power, and the glory, for ever.
 Amen

APPENDIX C

Suggestions for Further Reading and Study

Atwood, Dennis R. *Words That Shape and Form: A 40 Day Journey in Spiritual Formation*, Atlanta: Cooperative Baptist Fellowship, 2008.

Barton, Ruth Haley. *Sacred Rhythms: Arranging Our Lives for Spiritual Transformation.* Downers Grove, IL: InterVarsity Press, 2006.

Companions in Christ: A Small-Group Experience in Spiritual Formation. Participant's Book. Nashville: Upper Room Books, 2001.

Foster, Richard J. *Celebration of Discipline*, Revised Edition, San Francisco: Harper & Rowe, 1988.

Foster, Richard J. and James Bryan Smith eds. *Devotional Classics: Selected Readings for Individuals and Groups*, New York: HarperSanFranciso, 1993.

Foster, Richard J., ed. *The Renovare Spiritual Formation Bible.* New Revised Standard Version. HarperSanFrancisco, 2005.

Lane, George A. *Christian Spirituality: An Historical Sketch.* Chicago: Loyola University Press, 1984.

Merton, Thomas. *Contemplative Prayer.* New York: Doubleday, 1969.

Smith, James Bryan. *A Spiritual Formation Workbook: Small Group Resources for Nurturing Christian Growth*, New York: HarperSanFrancisco, 1993.

St. Augustine. *The Confessions.* Vintage Books: New York, 1998.

Willard, Dallas. *The Spirit of the Disciplines: Understanding How God Changes Lives.* San Francisco: Harper & Rowe, 1988.

The Book of Common Prayer.

www.ingramcontent.com/pod-product-compliance
Lightning Source LLC
Chambersburg PA
CBHW050759160426
43192CB00010B/1569